"*BeliefWorks* was ⟨...⟩ to go back to and reread or read to my husband. Thank you for assisting me on my journey."
—**Marti Woodward, Leadership Coach, Colorado**

"Extending the penetrating insights revealed in *The Power of Belief, BeliefWorks* offers even more. I highly recommend it."
—**Alan Nordstrom, Ph.D., Professor of English, Rollins College**

"Simple, straightforward, and immensely inspiring . . ."
—**Simeon Hein, Ph.D., author, *Planetary Intelligence***

"*BeliefWorks* is intensely insightful and infinitely useful . . ."
—**Fred Dearborn, LPC, Psychotherapist, Colorado**

"What a gift! *The Power of Belief* gave me the ability to look deep inside of myself and to recognize what's really going on from a totally different perspective. This is a must read . . ."
—**Donna M. Krebs, New York**

"The best! *The Power of Belief* ranks at the top of all the hundreds of self-help books I have read. In this world of 'fix me now,' it brings us back to the reality that this is a 'do it yourself trip' and gives us the tools to do it . . ."
—**Rita French, Montana**

"Ray's book is eye-opening. His simple yet powerful guide to unearthing your beliefs is a key step in making potent changes to your actions."
—**Cynthia Morris, CPCC, President, Boulder Coaches Alliance**

"Well thought out and incredibly effective. It is absolutely true: 'Real Change—One Belief at a Time!'"
—**Joe Scott, Tennesee**

Also by Ray Dodd:

The Power of Belief

BeliefW⚙rks

The Art of Living Your Dreams

RAY DODD

HAMPTON ROADS
PUBLISHING COMPANY, INC.

BELIEFWORKS™ is a registered mark of Everyday Wisdom.us Inc.

Hampton Roads Publishing Company, Inc.
1125 Stoney Ridge Road
Charlottesville, VA 22902

434-296-2772
fax: 434-296-5096
e-mail: hrpc@hrpub.com
www.hrpub.com

If you are unable to order this book from your local
bookseller, you may order directly from the publisher.
Call 1-800-766-8009, toll-free.

Library of Congress Cataloging-in-Publication Data

Dodd, Ray.
  BeliefWorks : the art of living your dreams / Ray Dodd.
      p. cm.
  Summary: "A guide to understanding and reprogramming the core
beliefs that drive your day-to-day decision making. Dodd offers
techniques for destroying old, self-limiting beliefs and creating new, self-
enabling ones"--Provided by publisher.
  ISBN 1-57174-472-X (5 x 8 tp : alk. paper)
  1. Belief and doubt. 2. Self-actualization (Psychology) I. Title.
  BF773.D63 2006
  158.1--dc22

                              2006005103

                    ISBN 1-57174-472-X
                    10 9 8 7 6 5 4 3 2 1
           Printed on acid-free paper in the United States

A Note from the Author

Many readers have asked me to include not only the what-to-do, but the how-to-do-it as well. As a result, *BeliefWorks* includes a number of stories used as examples to better illustrate the how-to.

In my work, people often come to me with a challenge and together we uncover long-standing hidden beliefs that are the key to finding the solutions they seek. This is an intimate process. To protect their privacy, I have fictionalized their stories and changed their names.

The remainder of the story-examples are from people who have given permission to have their names used, or well-known personalities whose circumstances are common knowledge through published works and the world-wide press.

—*R. D.*

Dedication

This book is dedicated to Susan—patient reader, advisor, true believer, partner, and fountain of endless love.

Your beliefs become your thoughts,
your thoughts become your words,
your words become your actions,
your actions become your habits,
your habits become your values,
your values become your destiny.

—Mahatma Gandhi

Contents

Introduction
Before We Begin

THIS IS A BOOK ABOUT MAGIC. *Real magic.*

In today's world, most magic is merely entertainment: digital computer graphics, special effects, and sleight of hand—a carefully orchestrated chorus of illusion. Yet each one of us, no matter how cynical or logical, wants to believe there is such a thing as real magic: the magic to change age-old conflicts into lasting peace; the magic to transform scarcity into abundance; the magic to spin our deepest desires and dreams into real-world reality; and most important of all, the magic to dissolve fear into love.

Perhaps you've encountered this sort of magic, or maybe you haven't . . . yet. Aware or not, day in and day out you experience the world in your own unique way, a one-of-a-kind perspective assembled by what you have agreed to believe. Your beliefs explain how the world is, but only how it is for you—your own personal virtual reality.

What we select to believe forms an intricate filter through which we perceive everything, a lens projecting a kaleidoscope of dreams, memories, and thoughts all wrapped up in an emotional point of view. What we experience in every moment is an interpretation, a mind-altering simulation, magically created by the amazing power of what we have chosen to believe.

The magic of belief is part of each and every one of us. Its dynamics cannot be changed, nor do they need to be. What is wonderfully interesting and full of extraordinary possibility is understanding how the human belief factory works and what it is capable of creating.

When I was a boy, there was a wooded area near my home that my friends and I played in almost every day after school. It was the field of my imagination. We could be knights serving the king and queen, secret agents rescuing the world from certain doom, or tigers silently stalking prey from the floor of the forest. And of course, being boys, we'd climb trees. From there I could survey the whole world—or at least what I thought was the whole world.

One thing I could see from high in those trees was the local waterworks. I saw large pipes, heard clanging and whirring sounds, and saw torrents of water going in and coming out. In the mind of a small boy, it was a magical place where they took the power and wildness of water and tamed it, transforming it into something useful.

In the same way, inside each one of us is a BeliefWorks. Without exception, we each take the untamed potential of belief and create a unique worldview that drives everything we do. From the raw energy of belief, we fashion a personal dream of life that touches every word we say, every thought we think, and every move we make. Our BeliefWorks manufactures the prism through which we see life and magically transforms what is into what we *believe* it is.

We cannot help but dabble with the magic of belief, yet we often wield its wand like the sorcerer's apprentice, unaware of its true power. Some perform black magic, stirring a cauldron of opinions anchored in fear, delivering bad news to themselves and anyone else who will listen. Others conjure up assumptions and opinions that explain everything so they can safely reside on a self-constructed island of what they know. And yet, many masterfully handle this tool of wizardry and use their beliefs as rocket fuel, propelling themselves to greater achievement, fulfillment, happiness, and personal success. Without regard for results, conscious or not, belief operates as the same predictable force for everyone, young and old, all over the world.

Recognizing the true power of belief and consciously putting it to work will uncover your ability to perform real magic, alchemy that miraculously affects the things you encounter every day: the work you do, the relationships you have with everyone you know, and even how you relate to the energy of money.

For many years, I have explored the idea that the most essential element in the process of personal and organizational transformation is understanding the true dynamics of belief. This has been a remarkable journey for me and many others who have traveled this path alongside me. *BeliefWorks* comes from hundreds of conversations I've had with people who asked me to assist them in creating positive change in their lives. Participating with me in exploring the world of belief have been artists, therapists, professionals, high-achieving business people, athletes, students, healers, and housewives—as well as companies and organizations from all over the world.

Holding *BeliefWorks* together is a simple framework of concepts and ideas. In addition to being supported by my own experiences as well as groundbreaking scientific research into how the mind works, *BeliefWorks* rests solidly on a system of thought I have found to be remarkably simple yet surprisingly effective when adapted to today's challenges. Many of this book's principles about the extraordinary transformation made possible by recognizing the true nature of belief come directly from the ancient wisdom tradition of the Toltec.

In the spring of 1996 I had the amazing good fortune to meet someone who changed my life so profoundly I was never quite the same again.

On a whim, I went on my first-ever trip to Mexico. Instead of finding myself on a sunny beach drinking salt-rimmed margaritas, I was convinced by a smooth-talking, charismatic Mexican named Luis to join his group on their journey to the mysterious pyramid ruins of Teotihuacán. According to Luis, the Toltec built the citadel of Teotihuacán approximately 2,000 years ago, around the time of Christ. His stories about the Toltec described them as an ancient culture considered to be men and women of knowledge by the farmers and artisans of the area. While they were not specifically a race or a religion, they practiced a unique way of life. According to Luis, they built the pyramid city of Teotihuacán as a place for community, a ceremonial seat of power, and a school for bringing selected groups of apprentices to personal freedom.

Luis claimed that most of us have lost our personal freedom. He explained that when we are young we develop a system of beliefs, a program that dominates our minds. If any part of that program is infected with other people's limiting fears about life, those beliefs become a parasite, *the Parasite of Fear*, depleting and draining us.

"If we develop an unconscious allegiance to fear, we lose our personal freedom," explained Luis. "We hold back so we can easily work within the system that domesticated us. We develop a habit of reacting and constantly defending what we know. We become a slave to an image of perfection that feeds the belief, *I'm not enough*. We are not free to choose what to believe because fear is in charge—not useful or true fear, but fear based on lies."

Luis said that the word *Toltec* means craftsman or artist.

"The Toltec thought your life, no matter what shape it was in, was your masterpiece, your art. They were *seers*. They saw that the mind is alive and one of its main purposes is to dream."

He went on to say that we each experience a waking daytime dream filtered through all the little agreements we make with ourselves that arise from our beliefs. By noticing our filters and cleaning them of unreasonable fear, we could awaken and become true artists of life.

"Teotihuacán means *The Place Where Humans Become as God*," Luis said proudly. "At Teotihuacán humans learned to live life consciously, with awareness of their own divine gifts, using their intent impeccably. In doing so, they regained their freedom, gathering enough personal power to create their own destiny."

Luis claimed the teachings of Teotihuacán were still alive, singing from the stones in the ruins.

Very few of the things Luis told me about the Toltec were supported by any archaeological or historical literature about the area. From what I could gather, the existence of the Toltec was indeed a historical fact. They inhabited central Mexico between the eighth and twelfth centuries and their influence was vast, representing the highest point of spiritual, cultural, and technological development in ancient Mexico. Luis's lack of accuracy bothered me, but he was very entertaining and I considered all of it good theater.

Luis told us about his teacher, a *nagual*. This word comes from Nahuatl, a language spoken by the people of Teotihuacán, the Toltecs and the Aztecs. In the Nahuatl language, nagual is the counterpart of *tonal*. Tonal is all the things that make up the solid everyday world, things that can be named. Nagual is the spirit that dreams, inhabiting the rocks, the plants, the creatures, and the humans. Everything that has a form, tonal, emerged from a place of potential without form, nagual. For the Nahuatl-speaking peoples, nagual is half of the reality we live in, half of our own nature.

Luis said the naguals were teachers who passed the Toltec lineage of special knowledge down to their apprentices. They taught their students certain concepts in order to have a productive conversation, but their real interest was exploring the unseen aspects of life—the appearance of creation as force and spirit. They understood that humans are obsessed with using words to describe every encounter, but the true experience of God is indescribable.

I asked Luis where we could find this nagual of his, but he refused to reveal his name or whereabouts. I didn't like that much either, but for the moment I accepted it as how things would be.

On the second day, while we were out in the ruins, a small, dark-skinned man approached us with about 20 people following him. He waved to Luis and opened his arms to greet him. Luis looked back at us and then strode forward to embrace this strange-looking little man.

Later that evening Luis's friend came to the salon in the hotel where we were all staying. He brought a cup of coffee, sat down, and balanced the saucer on his knee. I guessed he was about 40 years old. He had shoulder-length jet-black hair and was dressed in a polyester shirt and slacks—the kind of clothes you find in a discount store that look shabby after a few washings. He spoke so softly, his voice was almost a whisper. I paid very close attention to every single word, and yet I don't remember much about what he said that night. What struck me was the look in his eyes. They were liquid brown and induced in me the deepest peace I had ever known. What I do remember is that sometime during the evening everything in the room seemed to disappear. My world as I knew it collapsed, and for a moment I was alone with him, balanced on the edge of eternity.

Suddenly he stood up, made several strange gestures with his hands, and spoke once more. What he said changed my life in ways I never thought possible.

He was the nagual Luis had told us about. His name was don Miguel Ruiz, M.D., who a few years after we met wrote the international best-selling book *The Four Agreements*. Don Miguel's family, through an oral tradition, had carried the lineage of Toltec wisdom for centuries.

When Miguel was a young man and it was time for him to learn the tradition of his ancestors, he rebelled. Wanting nothing to do with the old people's ways, he went to medical school, became a surgeon, and embraced the modern world of technology and scientific knowledge. He settled into life and practiced medicine for many years. Then something very strange happened. As Miguel tells it, one night he had a terrible accident in his car. He remembers pulling two of his friends out of the wreckage. When he began to pull a third person out of the car, he recognized it as his own unconscious body.

Later this posed an interesting question for him, especially for a physician accustomed to dealing exclusively with the illnesses of the physical body.

"If I am not my body, and the mind that lives in my body, who am I?"

Through that experience Miguel decided to embrace the tradition of his ancestors, quit his medical practice, and follow a new path by learning the old ways.

After that night in the hotel at Teotihuacán, I was intrigued. I found out don Miguel was teaching in San Diego, California, and Santa Fe, New Mexico. I felt drawn to visit him. One trip led to another and for six and a half years I went to see him as often as possible.

At the time I was working as a corporate executive, managing the engineering operations for a large construction firm. I was successful, but nowhere in my formula for success was the idea that I could be happy. *Really happy.* I was on a spiritual path of sorts, and had even spent some time in a seminary, but I had long since given up believing I could find my heart's desire at work, or anywhere else in my life for that matter. I once had dreams for the future, but along the way I had forgotten them. I had assumed the role of victim, addicted to assigning blame outside of myself for all the things in my life that weren't going the way I thought they should.

My time with don Miguel, exploring the teachings of the Toltec, exposed me to a powerful framework for creating long-lasting change. Slowly but surely, I began to clearly see what I had agreed to believe. I discovered which beliefs were holding me back and learned simple yet powerful techniques to change them once and for all. Eventually I began mentoring others so they too could find "personal freedom" and put the power of belief to work.

A Little History

According to anthropologists, the Toltec Indians disappeared without much of a trace approximately 900 years ago, and so the story of the Toltec described to me by Luis and many others was endlessly fascinating, yet puzzling. Much of their account is missing from historical or archaeological textbooks. This is not totally surprising, however, considering that those who are victorious write history. What is known about the Toltec comes mostly from legend, oral teachings, and the few codex symbols (pictures) from antiquity that survived the onslaught of conquest during the Spanish exploration of Mexico.

Early in the sixteenth century, at the insistence of the Spanish governor of Cuba, the explorer Hernán Cortés pushed his way into Central Mexico looking for riches and lands for Spain. He and his small army advanced on the fabled city of the Aztec, *Tenochtitlán* (now Mexico City). Although Cortés was outnumbered 600 to one, the Aztec and their emperor Montezuma offered little resistance. In fact, Montezuma's ambassadors received Cortés with great ceremony. This was because Montezuma's scouts had returned to the emperor with terrifying reports of their encounter with the advancing army of Spaniards and their allies. To the Aztec scouts, the Spaniards were strange beings: half-man, half-horse gods with muskets. Montezuma was paralyzed by these tales. He thought the bearded, white-skinned Cortés was the legendary *Quetzalcoatl*, "the feathered serpent." An ancient Toltec prophecy foretold that Quetzalcoatl, a god descended from the sun and would-be king, would one day return and claim his throne in what is now Central Mexico.

Less than three years after their arrival in Tenochtitlán, the Spaniards dominated the empire of Montezuma and quickly suppressed the Aztec religion in their conquest of Mexico. To the Spaniards it appeared as if the Aztecs were dedicated to providing sacrifices to their frightening gods, and if these sacrifices were not offered, the gods would allow the sun to fail, bringing the world to an icy end.

The Aztec considered themselves descended from the ancient Toltec, but what the Spaniards saw was a terribly distorted Aztec version of an earlier Toltec culture. There is hard evidence that suggests the ancient Toltec were warlike, and yet there is conflicting evidence that implies that they were relatively peaceful for that era. Regardless, the Aztec had taken Toltec wisdom—*In Order to Summon the Divine You Must Give Your Heart*—and made it a terrifying reality atop the great pyramid temple at Tenochtitlán.

The Spanish priests were bent on eliminating a religion they viewed as the work of the devil. And they did it very effectively. One example is the monumental Metropolitan Cathedral in Mexico City, the crown of the main square—*El Zocalo.* The cathedral, built 53 years after Cortés defeated the Aztec, replaced *Templo Mayor*—the principal temple of the Aztec city, Tenochtitlán. In a demonstration of complete domination after most of Tenochtitlán was destroyed, the leaders of the Spanish church built the cathedral and main square directly on top of Templo Mayor.

Existing libraries of ancient writings and illustrations, passed down for centuries, were destroyed by Spanish priests and the Aztec's many enemies. In their conquest, the Spaniards treated the Nahuatl-speaking Aztec people, and the surrounding tribe of the *Mexica,* like animals. The enslavement and slaughter that followed plunged the land into centuries of darkness and drove all the surviving native spiritual traditions (including the Toltec) deep underground.

Toltec wisdom, veiled in secrecy, survived as oral knowledge for centuries. Passed on by naguals and their "parties" with instruction taking on the flavor of the teacher and the culture of the region, distinct lineages of thought emerged. Despite dark tales created by the European conquerors to suppress the Toltecs, and corruption by some naguals for personal gain, the essential knowledge was preserved and only resurfaced in the 1960s through the work of the late anthropologist Dr. Carlos Castaneda. Since then a legion of books has appeared about the Toltec and their teachings expressing a number of opinions and interpretations.

BeliefWorks

Regardless of the past, the essence of the Toltec teachings survives today, and their ideas, mythology, and practices provide a powerful yet simple approach to potent change. Adding it as a thread to the rich tapestry of *BeliefWorks* has provided an astonishingly effective tool to individuals and organizations striving for sustained well-being and excellence all over the world.

BeliefWorks begins with part 1, "Awareness Is the Solution," and reveals how hidden limiting beliefs may be influencing your decisions, driving your actions, and deeply affecting your experiences at every level. In the chapter "The Power of What You Believe," you'll discover a surprising new definition for belief, and you'll identify all the components that make what you believe so potent. In part 2, "Your Intent Is a Force," you'll explore the dynamics of taking action through a consciously constructed framework of agreements, new beliefs born from awareness, and I'll lead you through seven secret keys for unlocking the true power of belief.

Many people I talk to feel they have little power in their small corner of the world. I hear things like:

I'm tolerating so many things I just can't change.
I'm always doing for others but never for myself.
The world is too big and it's running my life!

Perhaps things haven't turned out quite the way you planned. Have you gotten off track? Maybe this book has found its way into your hands, in this very moment, because this is the message you have been longing to hear.

If you want to gather more personal power, and begin to realize your dreams, consider this. What you agree to believe about what has happened to you, and around you, is nothing less than an act of power. What you decide to believe manufactures the way you look out into the world, a bit of nifty magic that can launch you forward into an expanding universe of possibility or bind you, forever holding you back. You never lost your power; you just lost sight of it.

Belief is real magic, the magic to change obstacles into opportunity, transform disappointment into discovery, convert pain into pleasure, realize your deepest desires, and most importantly, assemble any point of view you choose. Discovering how to unlock the power of belief and erect an empowering structure of agreements in your private BeliefWorks is pure magic—a force you can use in each moment to bring into being what you want wherever you are. The possibilities are simply enchanting. By learning to harness the forces of belief and put them to work for you, you'll create long-lasting change, remarkable change, one belief at a time.

Awareness Is the Solution

Our truest life is when we are in dreams awake.

—*Henry David Thoreau*

The Tale of the Mango Tree

I WOULD LIKE TO TELL YOU A VERY OLD STORY. It is now just a myth, but if it happened, it happened before people explored all the places on the earth, discovered the wonders of science, or began to build machines to make life seem easier. In this time, people lived off the land and the sea, and they did not venture very far from where they were born.

This story begins with a clan of people living in the jungles of eastern India. They had been there as long as anyone could remember. They were hardworking and always busy—fixing this and improving that—and, oh yes, continually gathering food. There were many families in the clan—mothers, fathers, little ones, cousins, aunts, and uncles. Looking out for everyone was a small group called *The Old Ones.* They provided guidance when no one else could decide exactly what to do.

One pleasant summer day, a group of children ventured far from the village. Their job was to look for food. But like most children they played, teased each other, and only sometimes did what they were supposed to do. Quite by mistake they came upon a magnificent mango tree. It was very tall—perhaps 50 feet or more. The mango tree was heavy with fruit dangling from long stems. Up in the highest part of the tree were the most beautiful, large, and luscious mangos anyone had ever seen.

Two of the loudest and most adventurous boys climbed the tree first. They picked some of the giant mangos from the top of the tree, throwing them down to their friends on the ground. Everyone was laughing, eating, and having a marvelous time, covered with the sticky sweet juice of the mango.

Suddenly, a large snake came out of its hiding place coiled among the branches in the mango tree and began to wrap around one of the boys. The other boy watched in horror as his friend began to turn red and sputter, unable to breathe. He broke off a branch and hit the snake repeatedly but it did no good. Each time the boy gasped for breath, the snake squeezed tighter and tighter. Frightened, the second boy shinnied down the tree as fast as he could.

The others on the ground stopped laughing when they saw one breathless boy come down out of the tree and not two. They could hear their friend in the tree, moaning. And it was getting dark. Not knowing what else to do, they ran.

That night in the village, the Old Ones held a council to decide what to do. At first there was a lot of talk. No one in the room had seen what happened, but that didn't stop anyone from giving their opinion about what they assumed went wrong. After a while, the talk died down and for a long time no one said much of anything at all. Finally, the Old Ones ruled that some of the men would go, as soon as it was light, to get the boy. And the Old Ones made a law. No one was allowed to pick mangos from that tree ever again.

Several years passed and life went on in the village as it always had.

One unusually hot and sultry summer day, frayed parents who badly needed to find the children something to do sent them out to gather food. The children wandered through the jungle all afternoon, and just as they started to head back, they came across the very same mango tree. Spotting the giant fruit at the top of the tree, a slender young girl with a big toothy smile began to climb to pick the mangos. As she wrapped her arms and legs around the tree and started up, some of the other children grabbed stones from the ground and threw them at her yelling, "Lawbreaker! Lawbreaker!"

Crying and scared, she came down from the tree as fast as she could.

You see, the slender girl with the big smile was a baby when the law was passed forbidding anyone to pick the magnificent mangos. As a matter of fact, several of the children there that day had never heard of the law. But the children who threw the stones remembered their friend who had perished by the snake and knew they must uphold the law made by the Old Ones.

And so, many more years passed.

It was the dry season before the monsoon and it seemed to everyone that the progression of cloudless hot days, one right after another, might never come to an end. Mothers, wanting a little peace, sent the children out to look for food. After many hours circling the village keeping out of sight, the children once more came across the mango tree. The youngest boy and his twin sister, seeing the beautiful fruit at the top of the tree, yelled with delight to their friends, "Look what we found!" and began to climb up the giant fruit tree. A few of the boys picked up rotten fruit from the ground and threw it at them shouting, "Lawbreakers! Lawbreakers!"

Confused and frightened, the young climbers quickly came down from the mango tree.

This time, the boy and girl who got in trouble were not even born when the law was passed. And the children who yelled "Lawbreakers! Lawbreakers!" and threw rotten fruit learned about the law, not from any direct memory of the boy who perished by the snake, but from other children who were there that day.

And so, the same thing happened over and over again. And the fruit in the great mango tree was forbidden to be picked. The snake had long since moved on and by now had died of old age. The danger was gone, but the law was upheld, not by those who were there when the law was made, but by children who had learned from other children, who had learned from other children that you would be punished if you tried to climb the tree and pick any of the giant mangos. It was the law.

But after so many years no one could quite remember why.

The Power of What You Believe

EVERY BELIEF WE HAVE CONTAINS MANY AGREEMENTS—personal laws about what we should do, what we shouldn't do, and how everyone else is supposed to be. Like the story "The Tale of the Mango Tree," old agreements that arise out of what we choose to believe can intensely affect our lives. But we don't always remember how we came to our strongest beliefs. Even more confounding, many of the beliefs that powerfully guide our actions operate invisibly on a level far below what we are conscious of.

What you believe affects your relationships, where you choose to live, what you decide to buy, how you raise your children, the state of your health, wealth, and mind—as well as the work you do.

Belief impacts the dynamics of organizations, spawns or stifles innovation, muddles communication, defines religious faith, ignites terrorism, divides political opinion, shapes emerging trends, and drives every economy—close to home or halfway across the world.

With so much riding on what we believe, one question aches to be asked:

What is the true nature of belief and how did I come to all the little beliefs that have such a big effect on my life?

My own experience tells me that what we believe is far more than what we think is true. What is rational, reasonable, and occupies our thoughts is often no more than a set of opinions—judgments we constantly need to defend. What we really believe, what shines through regardless of what we tell ourselves and everyone else, spans far beyond the ever-expanding collection of information we store in our minds.

If someone asks you what you believe, you can probably come up with some pretty good answers—but are they true? Suppose you think you are a good, fair, and compassionate person. What happens when someone cuts you off in traffic, is rude in the checkout line at the market, or questions the quality of your work? Do you always act in accord with what you say you believe?

When we are stressed, put on the spot, or simply encounter the thorny realities of daily life, our behavior doesn't always line up with what we have told everyone we believe.

Mary was an elementary school teacher working in Denver, Colorado. Over a number of years she had developed a wonderful program of techniques for dealing with at-risk minority children. Her dedication and the program she designed generated so much interest that an educational foundation decided to film her teaching in the classroom so they could sell a video along with a textbook to other schools. When they filmed her working with the children, something surprising emerged. Every time she touched one of the children, she went to the back of the room and washed her hands in the sink! When she was shown the film, she was both surprised and embarrassed. She had no idea she was acting in that way. Later, she admitted that as a child raised in the segregated South she was exposed to constant prejudice, and although she hadn't recognized it, she had some real fears about dealing with black and Hispanic children.

The contradiction between what we say (or think) we believe and how we tend to act in the course of daily living is easy to explain. It's simply that we come to our beliefs through a lifelong series of multidimensional events, not merely through a progression of mental decisions. Belief is so much more than what we think is true. In fact, the first elements that form the structure of our beliefs appear long before we think with words.

The Way Beliefs Are Built

As little children, before we have language, we perceive the world with what I call our *tools of perception.* These are the five physical senses, emotion, and attention—the focus of our awareness.

YOUR FIVE PHYSICAL SENSES are hearing, sight, smell, taste, and touch. When you perceive physical phenomena like light, ambient aromas, background sounds, or warmth, your brain receives a series of complex electrical and biochemical signals, constructing a virtual model of the world.

EMOTION is a physical interpretation of an intelligent sense delivering information about the outer world and depositing it in our inner world. In a manner similar to the way our five physical senses deliver information to the brain, our truth-seeking sense—*intuition*—delivers signals that result in something we feel. Most of the time, we become aware of our emotions only when they are overwhelming us.

Big moments have big emotions, but if you take the time to notice, you are feeling something all the time.

Try this exercise: Sit down in a chair. Close your eyes and place all your attention on your breathing. Let your thoughts subside. For just a moment recognize how you are feeling in your body and in your emotions. Resist the temptation to define or describe in words how you are feeling. Now notice: Is what you are feeling always the same, or does it change ever so slightly from moment to moment?

Emotion is a membrane through which we feel our intuitive impression of the world. As compelled as we are to create a story about how we feel, words fail us. Can you describe your emotions the first time you fell in love, in enough detail so another person can know exactly how you felt? Can you use words to tell someone how you feel in this very moment so they can feel it, too?

No, of course not. It's hard to accurately describe your emotions with words and, if you take the time to notice, they change subtly from one instant to the next. Because you are always feeling something, every moment has an emotional signature, and big moments result in powerful emotional memories. The messages of emotion, without limited definitions using words, contain a wealth of information based on how you feel.

If you have knots in your stomach or you are suddenly breathless, those physical feelings are delivering important information about what is really going on with you, despite what you may be telling yourself. To grasp what your emotions are expressing, pay attention without trying to understand.

ATTENTION is the focus of your awareness, a search-light scanning what is before you. Attention opens your perception to what is going on all around you and inside you. You are surrounded by massive amounts of sensory data but you can only process a little bit of it at any moment. What you are aware of is what you focus your attention on. You learn and gather knowledge only by focusing your attention. Where you place your attention opens a channel of communication, but what comes through this channel is much more than light and sound. By placing your attention on something or some-one, you pick up on the inexpressible essence of what is happening in the moment. Have you ever had a sense or an instant insight about something before you had the ability to think about it? Have you ever walked into an unfamiliar place and immediately noticed something was wrong? When you were playing sports, have you ever reacted with your physical body faster than thought could begin? If you have, then you know what I'm talk-ing about.

The First Dream

When we are very small children, our first experi-ences and the program we receive from the adults around us form our initial impression of the world. Where we put our attention creates, for the very first time, our personal life-dream of how the world is for us.

When we are babies, we don't have language and so we absorb and begin to access the world around us using our tools of perception—the five physical senses, emo-tion, and our attention. Later, however, the adults who raise us want to communicate in a more effective way, and so they teach us language. Language is a complex and intricate code of sounds that have meaning. There are more than six thousand languages spoken on the planet, and each reflects the particular way its culture views the world. Take the ways we use words to express our love. In English we say *I love you* to our parents, our children, and to our beloved. In German you would say "Ich liebe dich"—*I love you*—only to your lover. To your children you would say "Ich habe dich gern"—*I'm happy to have you.*

Regardless of culture, location, or the language that is spoken, when everyone agrees on the meaning of the sounds, a real channel of communication is opened.

In order to teach us the code of language, adults needed to hook our attention. This may sound obvious but it's hardly trivial. We learn only when we pay attention. In order for them to pass their worldview on to us they need to control our most potent tool of perception, our attention.

Once we learn the code, adults tell us the name of everything we see. They tell us what the world is, what we will be called, how they are, and even how we are. They give us their opinions about everything. We are innocent and don't have much choice, but in order for us to absorb any of it, we have to willingly open the gate; we have to say yes; we have to agree.

Not one thing that is said to us, or modeled by adults, has any power over us unless we agree.

Of course we don't agree with everything. We selectively filter what everyone tells us. A family of six children living in the same household with the same parents will grow up to be six very different adults. Nevertheless, those early experiences, repeated again and again over a long period of time, make a deep impression on us. The agreements we make with ourselves about what happened to us become an important part of what we believe.

The process of having your attention captured, opening a channel of communication, learning the code, and making many little personal agreements creates your primary worldview—a personal life-dream created from the first time you paid attention. This is what the Toltec called *The Dream of the First Attention*, or what I call *The First Dream.*

Through this process, knowledge and particular points of view pass on from generation to generation. But some of what we learn is not so helpful. Like the story of the mango tree, what was true for one person at a particular time can become an opinion steeped in baseless fear handed down from father to son and mother to daughter.

As humans we naturally assemble information. To survive we need to make sense of it, and so we create stories about how one thing relates to another. But sometimes our stories become corrupted by opinions infected with fear that has no connection to any clear and present danger.

I an's new business had stalled. He was making furniture based on the philosophy of feng shui, the Chinese system of living in harmony with the natural elements and forces of the earth. He was making beautiful furniture and had a great website but wasn't selling much. Ian hired a consultant to develop a marketing plan but then found any excuse he could to delay putting the consultant's plan into action.

One day I asked him why he hadn't started to go out and make sales calls.

"I'm afraid I don't know enough. I don't think the people will buy from me because they will see I don't know what I'm doing."

"Is this a familiar thing, that you think you don't know what you're doing?" I asked.

Ian paused and closed his eyes.

"Yes, I've felt this way as long as I can remember."

"Who told you that you don't know what you're doing? Where did you learn that?"

"My father," he replied, almost whispering. "My father was always telling me to keep my hands in my pockets, keep my nose out of other people's business, and not to fool around with things I didn't understand."

"I'm curious. What was his father like?"

"Well, now that I think about it, my grandfather was always telling my father that he didn't know what he was talking about."

This is the way beliefs are built. Using our tools of perception, we begin to establish a channel of communication with the world. Before we have words, our experiences and the emotional signature of those moments impact our awake-dream. By using our attention for the first time, we learn the code of language allowing the adults to saturate us with their personal view of reality. A concept, an opinion, or an idea that comes from an adult in our lives, repeated again and again, eventually becomes a belief, but only if we agree. At some point, the words we learn as children begin to dominate our tools of perception. We become filled with a running internal monologue about how everything is that begins to hook our attention all the time. When this happens it's a very significant event. Now our BeliefWorks is running out of control. Our attention is captivated by the voice in our head that chatters on incessantly, an endless wellspring of knowledge, a program telling us about everything we believe.

Try this experiment. For half a day, carry an alarm that goes off every 20 minutes or so. Use your cell phone, watch, or PDA. When the alarm goes off, note what you are thinking about. Were you aware before the alarm went off how your mind was running and what it was engaged in?

By the time we become adults we have digested massive amounts of information, but our awareness has grown smaller with each passing year. We record only our big emotions and we need to describe those with words. Ninety-five percent of the time we perceive the world through what we see, what we hear, and through the voice in our mind. Our attention is imprisoned by the chatter of the mind with its opinions, assumptions, and declarations. The Toltec called this *mitote*, a commotion in our mind—a voice of knowledge filled with judgments. What is interesting is that the mitote that occupies the mind does not perceive much at all.

It is the interpreter of everything.

The word *belief* has its roots in words that mean "what you hold dear, what you love." What you believe is what you have embraced without doubt, investing every ounce of your faith.

The fabric of what you believe, woven by your tools of perception, is based on all your experiences, your decisions about those experiences, what comes through the channels of communication opened by focusing your attention, and years of exposure to the opinions and personal realities of the adults around you. Beliefs are holistic, energetic points of view—postures with a distinct perspective that always have an emotional signature.

Have you ever noticed that sometimes you have a strong emotion with no words to explain what is going on? That's because belief can sometimes be a wordless outlook, but it always has an emotional point of view.

What we believe inhabits our body, mind, and spirit. Belief bends all the input we perceive through our tools of perception. The words that populate our beliefs are simply agreements that defend and explain every point of view. In the cosmology of the Toltec, the human mind dreams 24 hours a day through a filter of all our beliefs and experiences, crafting a unique virtual reality, one that is different for every human being on the planet.

**A belief is a living dream with an emotional
signature populated by specific agreements
that define and defend its point of view.**

Have you ever met anyone who is nervous about things, can't trust anyone, and feels they have to watch their back? That outlook is a belief that knows, without a doubt, *I'm not safe.* How many little sayings, strategies, unseen behaviors, and stories do you think can come out of that point of view? You're right, there are thousands! Those are the agreements that define and defend its point of view.

The 2,000-year-old idea that the mind is alive and always dreams is more than a far-fetched notion of an ancient culture. These ideas are now well supported by cutting-edge scientific research into how the human mind works.

Your brain receives a continuous flow of signals about your body's chemical balance, temperature, and oxygen consumption along with a never-ending stream of nerve impulses. This raw data comes as biochemical bursts with attached electrical charges, and these impulses travel up and down an intricate web of nerve cells to your brain. Once a signal reaches your brain, the cortex itself assembles an even more complex arrangement of biochemical and electrical information.

Our brain doesn't inform us about this astonishing process. We simply notice it as pictures, sounds, tastes, textures, and tactile feelings—the product of our senses. We are aware and notice the world outside us through this amazing and mysterious process. But is it only about the world outside us? How about the world in us?

When you are asleep in your bed you experience a world of dreams alive with voices, sights, sounds, and for some, sensations like falling, smell, or taste. When you open your eyes in the morning you think, *I was dreaming and that wasn't real.*

But the part of the brain that is visual doesn't distinguish between awake and asleep. There is no separate mechanism dedicated to visual sensations while you are asleep and another while you are awake. The same visual cortex in your brain that allows you to see a sunset, your computer screen, or the faces of people you encounter while you are awake operates exactly the same way while you dream in your bed. The same storm of electrical and biochemical activity that produces the wildness of dream images while your physical body is motionless operates during the day, producing all the things you see.

Is It Real, or a Dream?

Our perception is based largely on sensory input and what we choose to believe. We experience a model of the world, not the world itself. The context we find ourselves in, and our opinions about what is going on around us, create the model. Simply put, our culture, how we were raised, our experiences, and all the things we believe to be true interpret everything we perceive.

Optical illusions are an excellent example of this. We don't see what we sense; we see what we think we sense. Our unconscious mind is presented with information, but what we are conscious of is a hypothesis, a simulation based on what we decide is true. Some optical illusions have two different interpretations depending on what you focus on: black vases in a white background or white faces in a black background; a figure of a young woman with her face averted or an old woman looking directly ahead; stairs going up or going down. What is interesting about optical illusions with different interpretations is that you cannot choose both simultaneously. One version is the shape you see and the other version is always unrecognized in the background.

Optical illusions using patterns illustrate the tendency of the mind to interpret what it cannot see. We literally "fill in the blanks" and superimpose what we think should be there.

To illustrate this phenomenon: One well-known experiment uses a standard-sized sheet of paper completely covered with a checkerboard pattern. On the left side of the sheet, in the middle, one third of the way in from the edge, is a small white circle with a dot in its center. On the right side of the sheet, in the middle, one third of the way in from the edge, is a small white circle with a cross in its center. Holding the sheet at arm's length from your face you can see the checkerboard pattern interrupted only by the two white circles—one with a dot in the center and one with a cross. If you stare at one of the circles with one eye closed and slowly move the sheet closer to your face, the other circle will disappear and the checkerboard pattern will become unbroken. There is a natural blind spot in the eye, a *scotoma*, and when the circle passes by it, the mind interprets what *should* be there.

People who are partially or completely blind sometimes suffer from the Charles Bonnet Syndrome. These patients, called "Bonnet-people," experience vivid visual hallucinations with their eyes open—odd things like complicated patterns, clowns, painted animals, or people who aren't really there. Often whole scenes will appear, at times life-size and at other times in miniature. In effect, these patients have an unusually large blind spot. Constant seeing actually stops the brain from creating its own pictures. Bonnet-people don't receive normal visual signals, so the brain makes up its own reality—the mind is free to dream.

We assemble our perception based on agreement— what we decide is true. If we determine beforehand what is important, then that is what we will see. Psychologists at Harvard University put this idea to the test in what they called "the gorilla-suit experiment." A group was instructed to watch a videotape of a handful of people playing basketball. The viewers were asked to count the number of passes made by one of the teams. Focusing on the number of passes made, more than half the viewers failed to spot a woman dressed in a gorilla suit who walked slowly across the scene for nine seconds, even though she passed between the players and stopped to face the camera and thump her chest. A few days later, the people who missed the gorilla the first time were asked to view the tape again without any other instructions. They noticed the gorilla immediately. The effect was so striking that some of them refused to accept they were looking at the same tape and thought it was a different version edited to include the gorilla.

In many ways, the world we experience is in us. Awake or asleep, what we see is only in our head. The cloud in the sky you saw yesterday was a simulation of reality. The light struck the retina in your eye and, through a complex biological process, produced a virtual image of the cloud in your mind. The cloud was only a dream.

What don Miguel said that night in the salon at Teotihuacán was, at the time, very difficult for me to comprehend. He said clearly, "Right now, you are dreaming." It took me years to understand what he meant. But now I know it's true. In this very moment you are dreaming-awake.

Your mind is always dreaming, producing a virtual simulation of what is distorted through a lens comprised of all your beliefs. If you'd like to begin to take control of your BeliefWorks and unlock its awesome power, consider these three powerful questions:

- *What have I agreed to believe, and how are my beliefs modifying what I experience?*
- *How can I recraft any limiting beliefs so I can get the results I want?*
- *Once I understand the true nature of belief, how can I put it to work for me?*

The Toltec had a simple yet elegant procedure for understanding the structure of belief, creating change, and then integrating this new understanding into every decision and action.

In the Toltec Wisdom tradition, the naguals (teachers) attempted to lead their apprentices to a plateau of realization they called personal freedom. They felt that most human beings weren't free—not because they were slaves or restricted by the laws of society, but because they were chained by the rules they had agreed to in their own minds. Rules that describe how life is. Confining rules that create conflict through unconscious judgments, opinions, expectations, and assumptions. Laws that prevent enjoyment of life's most succulent fruit, the juiciest mangos. They described personal freedom as the ability to awaken from an unconscious dream and live powerfully, moving through the world with conscious choice: an artist of life.

The path to personal freedom was a quest to break the chains of belief that dream the dreamer, invisibly running the BeliefWorks. The naguals assisted their students along this path by escorting them through three layers of understanding they called: The Mastery of Awareness, The Mastery of Transformation, and The Mastery of Intent.

The Mastery of Awareness

Simply put, mastering awareness is to awaken to the fact that the mind dreams night and day through a filter of beliefs, creating a unique experience of life. Without any recognition of how our beliefs project themselves into our virtual reality and modify our perception, there is little possibility of change. That's because we don't perceive things as they are; we perceive through our judgments.

**Real awareness is simply
perception without judgment.**

Awareness is 90 percent of the process of changing old beliefs and their respective agreements. In fact, awareness is the solution you may be looking for. Real awareness of the way you perceive the world is worth a thousand mystical experiences. Actions coupled with true awareness are acts of power, mastery, and co-creation.

Many times people come to me with a problem. They tell me all the little details about who said what and who did what. But the heart of the matter, what stands in the way, is often an underlying belief. Until the real issue, the core of the problem, is discovered, not much will ever change.

The Mastery of Transformation

Transformation involves taking an inventory of all the limiting beliefs and agreements you have discovered through awareness, withdrawing your investment of faith, and then reconstructing them. Transformation means radical change, like the metamorphosis of a caterpillar into a butterfly, or the process of alchemy where less valuable metals like lead are turned into gold. Real transformation is a deliberate act encompassing all the aspects of human consciousness and being—far beyond merely changing the thoughts in your mind. The Mastery of Transformation involves much more than changing what you think; it requires that you change what you believe.

Many problems are problems of interpretation. We want something or someone to be different so we are okay, even though we have little power to change it. The seed of those problems is almost always a belief, a point of view we agreed to that is now driving our actions. By re-creating a belief revealed by your awareness, and designing agreements that support it, you can change what you do and get a different result.

The Hillside Construction Company was having difficulty getting skilled carpenters. Local high schools had stopped teaching the trade and there were no unions training apprentices. Company staff had trouble filling positions. There was a pervasive agreement throughout the company: *We just can't find good help.* The outlook was grim and had the feeling of hopelessness. They had an outlook, a belief, that said, *We can't.* When they recognized what they had agreed to, and how it wasn't providing any solution, they rewrote their agreement to read, *We will recruit people with the right aptitude and train them ourselves.* Now they had an agreement that supported a different belief—*We can.* Acting on that agreement, they solved their labor problems in less than two years.

The Mastery of Intent

The Toltec described intent as the force that *Life* uses to manifest itself, and so your intent is the force you use to manifest your personal dream of life. You are always using intent whether you are aware of it or not.

Intent is volition, what you mean to do. Intent is the essential life force that precedes action, and it moves by absolute faith.

Creative energy attracts and manifests more of the same. Where you align yourself and how you use your energy are the direct applications of your intent. What you attract is what follows your intent. If moment to moment you are engaged in activities that leave you feeling stuck and going nowhere, then more of the same will follow. If you choose to put your energy into things that spark your passion, then that is what will populate your personal dream of life.

Describing intent is like trying to describe how you feel. You can't accurately define it with words, and yet it is a palpable force.

Mastering intent is the culmination of the art of living, using everything regained by recovering your awareness and transforming old fear-based beliefs to create a masterpiece of life.

Although there are three levels in this simple structure for change—Awareness, Transformation, and Intent—the core is awareness. Awareness is 90 percent of the process of changing self-defeating beliefs and taking firm control of your BeliefWorks. Until you notice how belief affects life on all levels—body, mind, and spirit—not much will change.

Complete awareness of a long-forgotten fearful belief is much like realizing you have been betrayed. The moment you see the naked truth, there is an extraordinary shift in your perception and suddenly everything changes.

In the movie *The Mask of Zorro*, a nineteenth-century Mexican nobleman, disguised as a masked swordsman, is the champion of the people against the tyranny of Spanish rule. Zorro (the Spanish word for "fox") is a thorn in the side of the ruthless governor of California. He is constantly harassing the Spanish troops. Unfortunately the governor discovers Zorro's secret identity. The Spanish guards attack his home, capture him, abduct his baby daughter, and accidentally kill his wife in the raid. Spain is conceding California to the Mexican general Santa Anna and the governor flees with Zorro's infant girl, taking her back to Spain to be raised as his own daughter.

Twenty years pass, and the governor returns to California intent on an evil plan to bring it under his total control. Upon learning of his return, Zorro escapes from prison, masquerades as a peasant, and prepares his revenge. Part of his plan involves training a young man, an orphan who helped him as a boy, to become the new Zorro.

Zorro's daughter, now a young woman, has a series of perplexing encounters with his old friends and servants. She doesn't understand why these people, in a land she has never visited, seem to know her.

When his training of the young Zorro is complete and his plan is in place, the elder Zorro invades the home of the Spanish governor and at the point of a sword has him reveal the truth to his long-lost daughter. Just by looking at her expression, Zorro knows she has realized the truth. Satisfied, he lowers his sword, saying only, "Now she knows."

In that moment his daughter sees her whole world collapse. Her reality, what she believed was true, has been revealed as a lie. When she becomes aware of the betrayal, everything in her personal dream of life changes. The man she thought was her beloved father is an evil murderer. The man she viewed as an insignificant peasant is her beloved father.

Awareness *is* the solution. Once you know what is really going on, 90 percent of the work is done. Once you are aware of what is true, and withdraw your faith, the transformation is almost complete.

By withdrawing your faith, I mean you begin to doubt what you once believed was true. Have you ever spent time with a group of people and then outgrown the things you did together? Almost everyone has this experience. What was once fun becomes unsatisfying. It just doesn't feel good to spend your time that way anymore. And so, little by little you stop showing up. You withdraw your faith.

Many people enter into this process driven by a desire to get to the solution, to fix a problem. They rush to transformation without any real awareness of what is going on and frequently fail to make long-lasting changes. It's much like dieting. Going on a diet, changing what you eat, and exercising so that the energy you put in your body is less than the energy you use will produce the result you want: to lose weight. That's transformation. But if you don't change the beliefs and personal agreements that drove your behavior in the first place, soon after the diet ends the weight will come right back.

Recognizing the power of what you believe and building on the cornerstone of awareness are giant steps toward consciously creating what you want. Detected or not, belief shapes everything. If you feel vaguely stuck or in a situation that doesn't seem to have a solution, understanding the force of belief may be just the magic you're looking for. You can put belief to work for you, first by starting with the foundation of awareness and then going further, exploring the remarkable promise of what you believe.

The Engine of Fear

LANCE ARMSTRONG IS A MODERN HERO. He has won the Tour de France, a grueling epic bicycle race that winds through the French countryside for three weeks in July each year, not once, but seven times in seven consecutive years. Lance's accomplishment is nothing less than miraculous. The Tour de France is a 2,300-mile pilgrimage with world-class cyclists from all over the world doing hand-to-hand combat, not only with each other, but with fatigue, distance, the French Alps, and unforgiving weather. It is one of the most difficult and longest sporting contests on the planet, an amazing physical, mental, and moral test.

What makes Lance's feat even more astounding is that at the age of 25 he contracted cancer and was given a mere 40 percent chance of survival. His battle back to the winners' podium in Paris along the Champs-Élysées, wearing the yellow jersey of the race leader—*le maillot jaune*—is now legend.

What drives such extraordinary achievement? By Lance's own account, in the early stages of his career, he was a young cyclist propelled by rage. Abandoned by his father, his mother gave birth at 17 to Lance and raised him alone. Everyone told her she would never amount to anything, but she had a different message for herself. She repeated one phrase over and over like a mantra: *Every obstacle is an opportunity.* His mother married again when Lance was three, but his new father was abusive, a man Lance would despise and never learn to respect.

When Lance started his career as an athlete, he used his old wounds and the energy of his fury as a competitive advantage. When he raced, he trash-talked, mouthing off to the other cyclists, showboating, and shoving his fists in the air. In the pack, he ignored the subtle jockeying for position that is part of the etiquette of European cycling. He wouldn't back down. Lance was a headstrong, stubborn, and insecure kid from the flat-lands of Texas with a big chip on his shoulder. Well into his racing career he dismissed the strategy suggested by his coaches—*conserve your energy for just the right moment*—and instead charged like a bull, head down, pedaling out of anger, never giving an inch. He was always on the attack. Lance was driven. Driven by an engine fueled with fear.

History is filled with extraordinary achievements by people who used the same fuel Lance Armstrong used in the beginning of his career to win races. Countless inventions, business empires, incredible feats of engineering, political conquests—even musical and literary masterpieces—have come into being because of the enormous drive of their creators—a drive with its foundation set solidly in fear.

Every action we take, large or small, pivotal or merely routine, is because of desire. We act because something is driving us. What propels us forward is an inner engine composed of our ideas, concepts, beliefs, and personal agreements. And the fuel for that engine is either love or fear. It's as simple as that.

As effective as anger and emotional pain may be as motivators, they eventually wear us down. The engine of fear leaves us unbalanced and stands in the way of long-lasting satisfaction.

Diane's goal was to take the invention she'd developed into the marketplace. She had put together an idea for diagnosing reduced lung function through an easy-to-administer specialized test that wasn't available to doctors. She wanted a sounding board and asked me to help her stay on track. Within a few weeks I noticed that the whole process was stalled. Something was holding her back.

"Why are you doing this?" I asked.

"I want to help people and I don't think doctors have the best tool for the job," she said with her arms crossed, looking at the floor.

She went on for almost an hour giving me all her reasons for launching her invention. But what she told me wasn't the real reason. I could see it, I could feel it, and I think when she decided to listen to herself closely, she didn't buy it either.

As we talked the problem through, Diane discovered something she had never noticed before. She was angry. Really angry.

Her husband was an executive at a biotechnology firm. They both had a similar education, but right after they were married she became pregnant, had twins, and stayed home to raise them. When the twins entered high school, she started feeling like she wanted to get back into the business world. She was brimming with ideas.

One night at the dinner table Diane started to tell her husband about some of her ideas. He listened impatiently and told her she was unrealistic.

"You don't know what you're talking about," he told her flatly.

He shot down every one of her theories. She expected him to be loving and supportive, giving her the benefit of his experience. Instead he was critical and impatient.

Diane didn't sleep at all that night. The next morning something was beginning to burn within her. Suddenly she had a strong desire: to prove him wrong. What had been driving her to put her invention on the market was her anger at her husband for not supporting her idea.

When we take a job, say yes to an obligation, or strive to accomplish our highest goals, what launches us into action? What often propels us forward is an engine fueled by our deepest fears.

Allen, the owner of a medium-sized law firm in Boulder, Colorado, was having trouble teaching confidence, poise, and patience to his newest lawyers.

"They're highly trained and very smart, but what I notice is a lot of people pursue advanced levels of education as protection."

"Really?" I asked. "What kind of protection?"

"The 'attorney at law' credential at the end of your name is a great way to be recognized and respected. The problem is, if that's a big part of why you did it, you're motivated by fear and not love of the work. You believe that you'll never measure up. I see this pattern more and more in the new lawyers we've been hiring. When they get in a stressful situation they lack real confidence, get defensive, and compensate by being arrogant, combative, and sarcastic."

What Allen described to me was an example of people spending an enormous amount of time and energy with one overwhelming and unconscious agenda: to be noticed and respected. His new attorneys are motivated, all right, but not always by passion or because they are excited to get to it every day. They are driven by fear. Fear they won't be accepted. Fear they are not enough. Fear they won't get it right. And it's not uncommon. What often guides our decisions about how to go forward is what I call "the prize"—getting what we think we deserve: attention, acceptance, recognition, and, most important of all, love. At home, in school, and even at work, what many folks are hunting for is not achievement, satisfaction, challenge, or inner peace. What they are hunting for is the prize.

Surveys about being happy at work list the things people want most out of work. At the top of the list is not money but being appreciated, having the opportunity to be creative, being recognized for their efforts, and having the ability to contribute something they consider meaningful. Number one on the list, what we value most, is getting attention—being recognized and appreciated. Of course, everyone wants some form of affirmation for a job well done. It feels good. But *needing* it is fueled by fear. When we absolutely require the prize, then obtaining it is the coal that keeps the fire stoked, and not getting it can ignite explosive drama.

You probably know someone, or know someone who knows someone, who has been laid off from their job in the latest business cycle of technology stock collapse or fallout resulting from corporate greed, offshoring, and downsizing.

A friend of mine was recently RIFed, a casualty of her employer's "reduction-in-force." She got an impressive severance package but instead of being relieved, she was devastated.

I went to see if I could cheer her up.

"Why are you so unhappy?" I asked. "You can take a year off and do whatever your heart desires."

"They don't want me anymore," she sobbed, broken-hearted.

Many people react like my friend when they lose a job, get fired, or are laid off. They don't feel wanted and experience the grief of loss. What made sense, what was solid and predictable, has come apart. Quickly, the first four stages of grief appear: anger, denial, bargaining, and depression. What may have been a business contract, *You give me something I want and I will pay you for it*, becomes personal. They are devastated and don't feel valued.

I've met many people who suffer for a long time after they lose their job, and it's not just about the money. If they suffer for months after being let go it's because one of the most important things about their job was being noticed and appreciated. Whether they were aware of it or not, one of their biggest motivators was the promise of getting the prize.

My first career was playing music, working in recording studios, and later running assignments for a recording artist management and music publishing company. It was an up-and-down life. I'd make thousands of dollars playing music for a few evenings and then not work for weeks. People in the entertainment business have a well-earned reputation for being brutally honest. To be successful and thrive, you had to have a thick skin to put up with rejection, and work harder and smarter. But I couldn't do that. I resisted looking closely at what wasn't working and I took any setbacks personally. Looking back, I didn't love the music business; what I loved was the idea of getting the prize. I wanted to be noticed, appreciated, and told I was good at it. And in moments when the prize didn't come, life was very hard.

I was running headlong at success and at the same time running away from something else: the truth. The truth was, I didn't believe I was worthy of the prize. I voiced an opinion to myself and anyone who would listen that I deserved it, but deep down what was driving me was an engine supercharged with fear.

What you believe either propels you into action or keeps you from taking action. This can be the biggest challenge in your life that is consuming you at the moment—like starting a new business, relocating far from home, ending a relationship, or changing careers. It can also be the smallest of things—like deciding what to make for dinner or where to meet friends. Either way, what you decide to do, what you choose to tolerate, what keeps you from going after what you want is an engine that drives you forward or runs on the lowest gears, dragging you down. *Something* is fueling your engine in every moment.

Do you know what's driving you?

Today, Lance Armstrong is a different man. His battle with cancer altered him forever. It changed his body, opened his heart, and deepened his fire for what he does. Visited by the Angel of Death, he understands with utter clarity that every day is precious and every step matters.

As he writes in his book, *It's Not about the Bike*, "It was the best thing that ever happened to me."

Lance made it through his ordeal sustained by the unwavering support of lifelong friends, family, and a cast of strangers who touched him deeply and became new friends. He is an inspiration, a worldwide symbol of what courage, determination, and hard work can accomplish. His cancer foundation, with its motto "Live Strong," has raised millions of dollars and helped hundreds of thousands of cancer patients with programs in communities all over the world. Today, Lance Armstrong is still a driven man—driven by passion, desire, new horizons, excitement, and discovery. More than ever before, he's driven by an engine fueled with love.

A World of Agreements

For centuries, in what are now India, Thailand, Sri Lanka, and Burma, elephants were used for transportation, war, and the hard labor of mining and logging. Wealthy kings owned many elephants, keeping them in immense stables and even forming elephant cavalries. The legendary general Hannibal used elephants to cross the Alps and battle the Romans 250 years before Jesus of Nazareth was born.

Capturing wild elephants was a dangerous and daunting task. Before an elephant could be ridden it needed to be trained, and before training could begin it needed to be broken. Old methods for taming elephants were brutal. Once the enormous animal was captured, a handler would start by chaining each foot to a nearby tree and leaving the elephant without food or water. The elephant would rebel—trumpeting, bellowing, stomping, and snorting in defiance. Finally, after three days or so, the elephant would give up. Having defeated it, the handler could approach the giant animal with food and water and training could begin. Eventually each elephant learned its job and went to work.

Once an elephant could be trusted, its handler would tie it down during breaks in the middle of the workday, not with shackles and chains, but with a rope around one foot and a stake driven into the ground.

This method of securing an elephant with a thick rope and stout stick pounded into the ground works amazingly well for restraining an 11,000-pound animal that can uproot trees and carry loads of up to half a ton all day long. A fully grown elephant can easily pull a stake out of the ground and roam free, but it rarely does. Why? Because the memory of its domestication is like a scar. The elephant doesn't tear the tether out of the ground the first chance it gets, *because it doesn't believe it can.*

A belief is an outlook, a living dream supported by agreements that define and defend its point of view. An agreement is a bargain, a deal, a pact you make with yourself. To agree is to simply say yes to a particular outlook. In order to develop a belief, we have to agree to its perspective, and in so doing we develop stories along the way that refine that point of view.

Of course, the elephant tied to a tether can't use words. But if it could, the agreements attached to its belief—*I can't*—might sound something like this:

The rope is more powerful than I am.

If I struggle, it will hurt and I'll go hungry.

Every one of us, in our domestication from child to adult, made certain agreements. These agreements are conclusions we come to in so many ways. Sometimes it's the environment or culture that surrounds us, the influence of an inspiring adult, a choice that comes from pain, or the result of years of education. Sometimes it's a promise we make to ourselves that emerges from a pattern in our life that repeats itself a thousand times. And sometimes it's the result of one mesmerizing and overwhelming event. Whatever it is, through our experiences we develop a belief system that is, in its essence, our mythology.

We have been taught that myths are either half-truths or legends about larger-than-life gods and goddesses battling it out using the forces of nature in supernatural ways. Myths are really made-up stories that explain life. In the same way, we all have a personal mythology that now guides us through our life that contains every belief, rule, and agreement we've assembled.

We each have a worldview supported by a body of personal myths associated with every event, every person we've ever met, and every situation we've experienced. Our mythology is the stories we tell ourselves and anyone who will listen about our personal history, our ideals, our opinions, our family, our friends, and even our enemies. Our mythology is the way we explain the world and our place in it, a mythology that forms a real and unmistakable boundary. That boundary is everything we know.

Some call this boundary an island of safety. I call it "the island of the known." On this island everything is explained. Whatever happens, we can assimilate it into something we know and have an opinion about it. And if we don't know, we assume we do and frequently develop an expectation about how it should be.

There are two very interesting things about the island of the known. First, it's almost invisible. It's a powerful influence but we're hardly aware of it. Second, it's a cage, and the builder and the guard are one and the same.

The island of the known is built by choice. Remember the story of the elephant? It decided, because of its experience, it could never break free. Because it has agreed it couldn't get away, it can't, no matter what is true in this moment. The elephant doesn't see that what is holding it back is merely an illusion, unshakably real and yet as solid as smoke.

Like the elephant, we too construct a perimeter, largely unnoticed, fabricated by thousands of bargains we make that define what is true and what is not. We make decisions, take action, and exhibit behavior every day, perfectly bounded by what we have chosen to believe.

Jesse and Sarah were having problems with their teak furniture business.

It all started five years earlier. That September they went on vacation and stayed at a quaint little bed and breakfast along the shore in North Carolina. Every morning they had coffee on the porch and watched the sun rise over the ocean. The porch was furnished with exotic teak furniture from Indonesia.

They fell in love with it. Within six months they took a trip to Indonesia and brought back a variety of teak furniture. What they didn't keep, they quickly sold to friends and neighbors. They loved the furniture and liked the idea that, by importing and selling it, they could support a local economy making natural products half a world away.

They started buying trailers of furniture, selling it at home and garden shows. One thing led to another and soon they had eight teak furniture stores along the east coast of the United States.

Sarah and Jesse weren't happy with how the business was going. They didn't like maintaining the stores, dealing with the intricacies of importing, or coping with employee problems.

Jesse: "I'm not sure how I got into this. I guess I thought it might be fun. Maybe it was at first, but now I'm not even sure I care about furniture. I feel like some-body I don't really know got us involved in this."

Sarah and Jesse didn't think that what the business had grown into reflected their values. Sarah dreamed of providing natural furniture to beautify people's environ-ments and creating a "village" of employees and suppli-ers who would reap prosperity for their families in order to create a more healthy and peaceful world.

They were convinced that by stepping back and refo-cusing their priorities they could enjoy importing teak furniture once again.

Together we explored their situation. What we discov-ered was surprising.

First, very few of their employees shared their stated values. Their salespeople frequently misled customers. Eventually Jesse discovered that several of them were stealing and couldn't be trusted. Their manufacturer in Indonesia was always late delivering furniture. They fre-quently sent shipments that were short of merchandise, and what did come was often damaged. Sarah had to refund people's money and they were losing customers because promises couldn't be kept. Jesse told me they struggled to pay their bills and he often woke up in the middle of the night, worrying.

I heard Jesse admit that he thought all this was normal.

"It's impossible to get good help, suppliers can't be trusted, and so you deal with it the best you can."

I asked Jesse how the situation felt to him, not just what he thought about it.

"It's like being in an earthquake—at any moment it could all come tumbling down."

"Is this a familiar feeling?"

He paused a moment, looking up at the ceiling, and then said slowly, "Well, come to think of it, I guess it is.

"When I was 12, I came home after school one day and found my mother lying on the kitchen floor. She'd had a seizure and collapsed. After that, nothing was the same. Everything was up in the air: how we would pay our bills, where we would live, even where we got our next meal. It was terrible. I remember for a long time making every decision thinking at any moment everything could fall apart. I never felt safe."

Thirty years later Jesse was still making decisions bracing for the moment when everything would fall apart. At first the business was fun, but as soon as it got serious and stressful he made choices fueled by the engine of fear. He dismissed his intuition and hired whomever he could get. He signed leases out of desperation. He made deals that didn't feel right just to get furniture in the stores. Every decision he made supported his invisible belief that everything was in danger of tumbling down. Although he said he wanted to nurture an enlightened business culture, his real values were cemented solidly in fear.

Nobody made Jesse *do* anything. In fact, every move he made was fueled by old agreements—agreements profoundly influenced by what he believed was true.

Once Jesse and Sarah recognized that what they had created was largely by choice, they dismissed their problem employees, closed the stores that were struggling, and began searching for key employees and suppliers who would support the values they dreamed of creating. They downsized their business, eliminating many of their problems, and made more profit than ever before.

Except in the most extreme circumstances, everything you do is because you agree to it. Where you live, the job you go to, the people who are in your life, what you tolerate, the last argument you got into, even what you ate today—all of these are agreements you made with yourself that align perfectly with what you believe.

This is such a powerful and yet simple concept. You have very little control over what other people do. You don't have absolute power over what happens to you, but where you are commanding and have complete and unchallenged authority is in what you decide to believe about what happens to you and around you.

> **Where we have complete and unchallenged
> authority is what we decide to believe
> about what happens to us and around us.**

We choose what to believe and those choices craft the reality that propels us forward or holds us back. What deeply affects our lives, right now in this very moment, is what we have agreed to believe—whether we notice it or not.

Isaac is a franchise owner in his mid-50s. Originally from Missouri, he now lives in southeastern Colorado. When Isaac was 13 years old, his father died of a brain tumor. Neither his mother nor his father told him about his dad's illness, but for years he had the feeling that something was wrong. One day his father and mother left for a trip in the car. His dad never came back.

After his father died, Isaac was angry.

Why didn't they tell me? This isn't fair. How could he abandon me? Why would God take my father?

The only world Isaac knew collapsed and he was in a lot of pain. The very first unspoken agreements we have with our parents—*You will take care of me; I'm safe with you; you will always be there for me; you will love me as I am*—were forever broken. Grief came but he would never let it finish. His mother wanted him to become the man of the house after his father died, but he couldn't move past feeling abandoned and never took charge.

Instead, Isaac made an important agreement with himself.

I will never hurt this way again. If God can do things to people like this, then there is no God—at least not a God I want anything to do with.

Isaac fell into 30 years of alcohol abuse, three failed marriages, and a never-ending progression of new-start careers.

His father has been gone for almost 40 years now. None of this was ever about his father. In a masterful stroke of self-importance, Isaac decided what was true, devised a personal book of rules—judgments he nurtured about himself, God, and everyone else around him—and kept it alive for all those years.

When Isaac developed a clear awareness about the agreements he made so long ago, he stopped using his father's death to abuse himself and gave up his need to be right about his old point of view. When he did that, the world he created collapsed. Because his judgments wouldn't hold up without his constant investment of faith, they dissipated like fog being burned off by the hot sun. Isaac's mythology was a self-fabricated universe based on lies he had agreed to believe.

For the first time in his life Isaac is allowing himself to care, to be loved, and, most importantly, to love himself. As he says, "I feel like I've awakened from a bad dream."

Many books, magazine articles, and speakers purport to have the key to happiness. They hook our attention with the promise that we can be happy all the time. But is it *really* possible to be happy all the time?

The truth is we don't normally experience perpetual bliss if our pet dies, we lose our job, we become ill, or a loved one passes away. Our natural response is: *This doesn't feel good.*

In difficult times, our emotions can bring us the gift of growth and healing, but when we don't allow the feelings to run their course, and instead create a story that sustains the emotion long after the event, we can suffer for a very long time.

Happiness isn't always being in that joyful place. *Happiness is not-suffering.* We don't always get what we want, but making up a poor-me story perpetuates the emotion and causes suffering. If we are suffering it is often because what we have agreed to believe is based on lies.

To be happy requires choosing a perspective that doesn't make you suffer.

The expectation that everything is always going to go well is unrealistic. We can't always affect the physical reality of what happens to us or around us, but we can agree what to believe about it. What we decide is true impacts the essence of every experience.

An example: As we age, the normal reasons to be happy are not always as plentiful. Common reasons to be happy—a romance, a new job, a raise in pay, or satisfaction brought on by achievement—are harder to come by as the body gets older. Many people are happy, but only for a particular reason. And if there is no reason, they aren't necessarily happy or at peace. But that's just an agreement that limits real freedom.

Is it possible to decide to be happy for no reason at all?

The realization that almost everything you do and everything you believe results from your agreements is good news. It's good news because it means you have all the power you need.

For example, if we interpret what happens to us and fabricate a victim story, and believe it's true . . . then change is impossible. But a victim story and the complaining that goes along with it are simply choices. We can always agree to choose something else to believe.

Most of us are never forced against our will; we are not victims of anything except our own choices. Even when people really are victims of a crime, such as a break-in, what is true is: There was a break-in, something was stolen, and the emotion the moment the break-in was discovered was authentic. The rest is a made-up story.

Even when people are victimized by circumstances far beyond their control, they still have the power to agree what to believe about what is happening to them and around them.

Dr. Viktor Frankl, a psychiatrist from Vienna, Austria, and author of *Man's Search for Meaning,* was a prisoner at Auschwitz—a Nazi concentration camp in Poland during the Second World War. All the prisoners in the camp faced constant hunger, cold, unimaginable brutality, and the threat of death in almost every moment. While Dr. Frankl was fighting for his own survival, he made a startling discovery. In this very worst of circumstances, those who decided they had something to live for, a purpose to be accomplished, seemed to thrive, while those who had lost all hope quickly perished.

Despite the awful surroundings they could not escape from, one thing could never be taken away—the ability to choose an attitude and agree to a point of view, despite what was happening, that supported life and hope.

You create the life you experience every single day. Whether you are held back by an invisible or insignificant restraint, or motivated by investing all your faith in the belief, *I Can!* you are the creator of the dream of your life and the one with all the power.

Only *you* have the power to agree what to believe.

You Are Living **5** *Your Dream*

ONE DAY I WAS STANDING IN THE CHECKOUT LINE AT THE supermarket reading a national lifestyle magazine. The headline on the cover blared: "When is your ship coming in? The ONE WAY to find out what's keeping you from what you really want."

Intrigued, I opened the magazine and began to read the article. In the very first sentence, the writer asked: *What is the one thing keeping you from living your dream?*

It's a good question. It's a great question. But perhaps it's not the *right* question.

First of all, what is your dream? Is it something you want but always seems to elude you? A faint desire that occasionally distracts you until you dismiss it and go back to your *normal* life?

Conventional logic implies that you must be doing something wrong if what you really want, your dream, isn't coming together right before your eyes.

Maybe you aren't doing anything wrong at all.

The ancient Toltec claimed the human mind is alive and one of its main purposes is to dream. They described beliefs as filters through which the mind dreams; thus the essence of our experiences is crafted by what we have agreed to believe. Today, quantum physics, cutting-edge neuroscience, and countless spiritual traditions old and new tell us the very same thing. We are the masters of our own reality, our virtual assessment and judgment of life's richness, our waking life-dream.

You *are* living your dream! Perhaps a better question to ask is: *What is the dream I'm living, and is it serving my highest good?*

To notice how your personal filter of beliefs creates the daily life-dream you are living requires awareness of what you actually believe (not what you'd like to believe) and how that distorts or enhances what you experience.

What we think we believe is often an opinion we are addicted to defending, not what is really driving our behavior.

Okay, how do I discover what I actually believe? What does it take to reveal the underlying invisible agreements I made long ago that are now running my life?

It's not that difficult. Just look around you.

- *Do you have enough money or very little of it?*
- *Does your love life feel like quicksand or a universe of infinite possibility?*
- *Do you have a large, loving group of friends or hardly any at all?*
- *Are you are excited by the work you do or do you just tolerate your job?*
- *Do you like where you live or do you feel stuck?*

These things and more reflect your beliefs. Your perception, your actions, and your reactions are the direct result of what you have agreed is true. The endless progression of dialogue in your mind is filled with agreements that align perfectly with what you believe.

What is even more revealing about what you believe is that everyone in your inner circle, the people you select to share your most private moments with, is a character in your movie reading off your script.

If you want to know more about what you actually believe, look at what and who are in your life.

Notice what happens in your routine every day. You are the main character in your movie and the people whom you deal with on a daily basis are minor characters reading from a script you wrote, a script with dialog and motivation supporting whatever you believe.

A movie director looks for the underlying motivation along with dialog and action to create a scene. That is by intention. When we are unaware of our own motivation, we may think we are in conflict with our handpicked supporting cast, but in fact we are not.

Alison felt disconnected and stuck. She desperately wanted to put some fire back into her 25-year marriage and in her work.

Before we start to work together, I always ask people to write down their story—what they would say about themselves to a stranger they had just met. I ask them to be honest and write about who they think they are and what they believe is true. What is fascinating is that everyone lies to me. Not intentionally of course, but I rarely get the truth. What I get is a tall tale that accurately reflects their unique distortion of reality and their ignorance of the hidden beliefs that are running everything.

Alison wrote that she was one of five children—four boys

and one girl. Her father was distant, but only to her. She remembers he seemed much more interested in her brothers. She was treated differently even though she was always trying to prove that she could do anything they could do.

In college, Alison met David. He told her she was "the one," the woman he had been looking for all his life. He was flattering and passionate, and made her feel special. They married after college and were happy for a few years. Alison tried hard to please David but he wanted more than she knew how to give. He always wanted to know where she was going and whom she was with. He even convinced her to quit her job, abandon her career, and stay home with their young son.

Now that her son was in high school, Alison wanted to go back to work and revive her passions, but she didn't quite know where to start. She felt at odds with David and the long road they had traveled together.

David gave her what her father hadn't. He told her she was special. She desperately wanted the man in her life to appreciate and recognize her. When she was a teenager she made a very important agreement with herself. Based on how she thought her father saw her, she decided that there must be something wrong with her and she wasn't good enough. Without noticing it, she selected a man who carried the very same belief about himself. His own personal agreements made him jealous and controlling out of fear because he didn't believe he was good enough, either.

Her husband, David, wasn't a problem or an obstacle. He was the perfect character reading carefully tailored dialog authored by her belief about herself and all her old agreements about her father. He was a minor player in her movie—her personal dream—supporting her decisions about life 100 percent.

This very same dynamic exists not only in our personal lives, but in businesses and other organizations as well. I am often contacted by companies that want to create a different business culture centered on values they feel are important and empowering. To do that and create long-lasting change, we first need to identify what underlying beliefs and agreements impact everything. What I find over and over again is that although things are not the way we want them to be, they are exactly as we have created them.

On a recent trip to Sacramento, California, I visited two air-conditioning service companies to observe their corporate cultures and help them craft the values they wanted to instill within their organizations.

The first company I visited was owned by Allan, a retired United States Air Force major, and his wife, Susan, also retired military. Susan was in charge of the office and sales, and Allan ran the operations. Allan was in his mid-50s. He had an erect posture and athletic build, and looked me straight in the eye when he spoke. When I met him for the first time, I got the sense he was fair but wouldn't tolerate any excuses. It was a short interview, concise and to the point.

I spent the rest of the day with his employees. They were clean-cut, in good physical shape, wore dark blue pants and light blue shirts, and addressed me directly. Some even called me sir! Everyone I observed dealt with customers in a friendly and efficient manner. Their offices and fabrication shops were clean and well ordered.

Allan wanted his employees to be more decisive, make judgments out in the field, and stop waiting for orders. He and his wife wanted to retire and sell the firm—preferably to one of their employees who would take the initiative to run the company.

Everybody Allan and Susan hired was an extension of themselves. Their employees were military, erect, and conditioned to respond to orders. Everything was ship-shape. Even their clothes looked like Air Force enlisted-personnel uniforms. The employees weren't acting independently because they were the supporting cast reading off Allan and Susan's script.

The second company I visited was owned by Bill, a portly man in his early 40s who had started several air-conditioning service companies throughout California and was now living in Ensenada, Mexico. He had come back to Sacramento to manage the office because his hand-selected manager had quit and the operation was struggling.

In my interview with Bill, he launched into an hour-and-a-half monologue about real estate, growth, politics in California, lack of business regulation, his ex-wives, and his competitors. He was funny, engaging, and had an opinion about everything. He used his hands to talk and raised his voice to make a point.

The open office area at Bill's company was like a war zone. There were unsorted piles of paper everywhere. The dispatcher yelled out commands. Nobody got up to take breaks and there was food on every desk.

I liked the people there. They were dedicated to doing a good job but were constantly under siege. Emotions were running very high.

Bill came out of retirement to try to rescue his company. He wanted the operation to run smoothly so he could bow out of the day-to-day management and go back to Ensenada, but miscommunication was routine and the office was suffering from daily emotional flare-ups. Promises to customers weren't being met and the whole operation was in a constant crisis mode. All any-body could do was put out one fire and then move on to the next.

Bill's operation was a perfect reflection of himself. His own office was a mini-war zone with food and piles of paper everywhere. He was volatile, emotional, and lapsed into crisis management from moment to moment.

Making real changes and harnessing the force of belief require undeniable awareness that you are living your dream and noticing that whatever is continually going on around you is not some odd coincidence or a run of bad luck. What is keeping you from living your dream? Nothing! It just isn't true that you are not living your dream.

You are precisely living your dream, and the people in your inner circle are handpicked players directly supporting what you believe.

Remember, all beliefs are supported by agreements that you make. Recognizing that you are living your dream can be a very powerful thing. Rather than asking, *What is the one thing keeping me from living my dreams?* take a moment and ask yourself:

- *What have I agreed to and what is that creating?*
- *How is my own unique perspective driving my decisions, actions, and reactions?*
- *Does my outlook ever keep me from realizing my deepest desires?*
- *Who are these people in my life and how are they reflecting what I believe?*

Noticing this dynamic can be startling. When you decide to make real and fundamental changes, many times the characters in your movie—beyond your immediate family—also need to change. The Buddhists have a wonderful saying, "Wherever you go, there you are." The world doesn't change, you do. When you change, your life-dream changes and so do the characters in it.

The art of living your dream is more than getting everything you desire. It starts with noticing how people live in a virtual reality that has nothing to do with you rather than reacting, taking things personally, and defending yourself. The art of living your dream is noticing that every mind dreams. Acting accordingly, you recognize the authentic power you have and deliberately begin using all the elements of belief.

What we believe is filled with remarkable promise. There are six billion-plus virtual realities on our planet creating what the Toltec called *The Dream of the Planet.* That collective dream spawns art, innovation, invention, emerging trends, and new cultures as well as violence, intolerance, prejudice, pollution, addiction, crime, and war.

We are all in this together, but many live in a world of wounds. Fear sells, and those who preach the gospel of fear garner the most attention. The media often converts information into fear. Fear is routinely spun into best-selling books, blockbuster movies, the hottest video games, and the newest music. And yet, the dream of the planet changes when even one dreamer awakens. By living your dream as an artist of life, consciously taking control of your BeliefWorks, you become an anomaly: a new strain of virus in the old program.

You are living your dream, a perfect reflection of what

you believe. Once you notice that and assume full responsibility as the dreamer of your life, a whole new world of possibility will magically open right before your eyes.

The Gates of Lucid Living

Close your eyes and remember a face you saw today. It can be someone you know well, someone you met who made an impression on you, or simply a face from a magazine or movie. Now open your eyes and write down a description of the face. Put in all the detail you can remember.

If you were to read your description to someone else, would they be able to see the face clearly? If they knew that person too, would they recognize who it was? Which is more accurate: your visualization with eyes closed or the written description?

We have a whole world of perception inside us that has nothing to do with the words in our mind. Describing how we feel or telling someone about the dream we had last night can never come close to the essence of that experience because the intellect, the rational mind that thinks in words, is not a tool of perception. It's a tool of analysis.

Experiencing insights or intuition, and then describing what we perceive with words, can actually impair those experiences. Research scientist and psychologist Jonathan Schooler of the University of Pittsburgh calls the use of words to try to define pure perception "verbal overshadowing."

When you attempt to explain a perception such as seeing a face, the left hemisphere of your brain, which thinks in words, *overshadows* the right hemisphere of your brain, which stores your visual memory.

In an experiment to illustrate how this works, Dr. Schooler showed volunteers a 30-second video depicting a man robbing a bank. After watching the video, all the volunteers spent 20 minutes on an unrelated task. At that point, half of the group was asked to write a detailed description of the robber's face. These volunteers were encouraged to focus on each of the criminal's facial features and jot down their memories. The rest of the group spent their time on a second task unrelated to the video.

All the volunteers then tried to identify the robber's face from an array of eight photographs. About one-third of those who wrote a description picked out the correct face. But two-thirds of those who didn't write a description picked out the robber from the photographs. The memories of his face were much poorer among eyewitnesses who tried to describe what he looked like shortly after seeing him, compared with those who didn't try.

What Dr. Schooler and his researchers discovered is that in moments when a solution is best derived by making split-second decisions in a fluid, nonverbal way, the act of examining something with logic resulted in a substantial loss of meaning. Analyzing everything with the rational mind resulted in a significant reduction in the ability to recognize what was really going on.

The concept of verbal overshadowing challenges the

notion that language lies at the core of understanding. Dr. Schooler: "Various forms of inexpressible knowledge are best served by avoiding the application of language. Words sometimes get in the way."

There are lots of theories about the configuration of the human brain—that it's a hologram, that it consists of layers starting with a primitive brain containing our emotions and instinctual responses, that it's an organ housing only a part of our consciousness, or that all cells are energy and matter programmed for a specific purpose and can be reprogrammed.

The most popular view is that the brain has a distinct physical structure divided into two hemispheres: the right hemisphere, which is our more imaginative and intuitive side, and the left hemisphere, which is our more logical and analytical side. The arrangement of the brain reflects what the Toltec called the tonal and the nagual, or what I call the *language mind* and the *dreaming mind*. The language mind is our reason, our ability to use words to analyze, assess, and judge what our tools of perception notice. The dreaming mind perceives without words and records an impression of the inexpressible essence of things.

The language mind is your reason, the ability to use words to analyze, assess, and judge what your tools of perception notice. The dreaming mind perceives without words and records an impression of the inexpressible essence of the moment.

The language mind is an enormously useful tool. We make up stories using words that help us make sense of things. The language mind is an evolutionary development that has helped us survive.

If you are hiking through the forest and suddenly encounter a ferocious bear, your animal nature goes into an instinctual fight-or-flight response. Your language mind, your intellect, decides what to do about it in order to survive.

We come up with solutions expressed in words in order to understand what is happening and to feel safe. But what if, in our process of learning to be a man or a woman, this tool of analysis becomes polluted with fear that has no solid ground?

In fact, this happens to all of us in one way or another throughout the making of the First Dream—our domestication as children. When this occurs, the voice speaking words in our heads becomes a running discussion dominating our attention so completely that the myriad other ways we perceive are hardly noticed.

Take a moment. How often is your attention captivated by the voice in your mind? If you did the exercise in chapter 2—carrying an alarm that goes off every 20 minutes or so to note what you are thinking about—you discovered that it is most of the time. The mind's chatter constantly describing what you know severely impairs your perception. Your tools of perception—the five physical senses, emotion, and attention—are overshadowed by the often fear-filled voice of knowledge and its constant presence in your thoughts. Your internal dialog, what the Toltec call mitote, is a never-ending clatter drowning out the essence of the moment.

When the language mind becomes overly dominant, perception can be terribly distorted. To illustrate, Dr. V. S. Ramachandran, author of *Phantoms in the Brain*, recounts one story about a stroke victim confined to a wheelchair. His patient suffered from *anosognosia*, a denial syndrome occurring in people who have neurological damage, usually caused by a stroke to the right side of the brain. Denial patients are blissfully unaware that the left side of their body is completely paralyzed. The right hemisphere of our brain, which controls the left side of our body, is our more imaginative and intuitive side. When there is damage to the right hemisphere, the left hemisphere (responsible for language, comprehension, and meaning) attempts to assume complete control.

One day Dr. Ramachandran visited his patient.

"Why are you here?"

"I had a stroke," the patient replied.

"Can you walk?" asked Dr. Ramachandran.

"Oh, yes."

"Can you clap your hands?"

"Of course!"

The denial syndrome in stroke-damaged patients illustrates in an exaggerated way what is true for all of us. We are flooded with an overwhelming barrage of sensory input that we need to incorporate into our normal view. To fit it into our unique belief system, we devise a story that helps us make sense of the world. Our language mind takes input that doesn't fit on our Island of the Known and either ignores it or, to preserve stability, distorts it by squeezing it into our existing structure. To do this, we unconsciously lie to ourselves and ignore what is.

To fire up your BeliefWorks requires much more than just the language mind. The dreaming mind—the part of you that is aware, notices, and perceives without words— needs to be on equal footing with the language mind.

The dreaming mind can be enormously useful. Albert Einstein claimed that one of his main theories about relativity came to him, not through rational thought, but in a daydream where he imagined himself riding on a beam of light.

Your dreaming mind can be used to get answers to questions, inventory worn-out beliefs, communicate more effectively, rehearse a new perspective on your life, or achieve deep relaxation and peace.

How can I balance the language mind with the dreaming mind?

The first piece of the puzzle is revealed through the ancient art of lucid dreaming.

Stanford University dream researcher Dr. Stephen LaBerge has been studying the effects of lucid dreaming for more than 25 years. Lucid dreaming occurs the instant you recognize you are dreaming when you are asleep. In the moment you realize you are dreaming, you become lucid and clear about what is happening. Lucid dreamers, unlike normal dreamers, can make choices in their dreams.

At the beginning of his research, Dr. LaBerge found this to be an intriguing idea. Buddhist tradition, along with many other ancient cultures, described life, both awake and asleep, as a dream. But inside the concept of lucid dreaming lies a paradox: *How can you be conscious and unconscious at the same time?*

What Dr. LaBerge discovered is that consciousness is not always body-specific. If our awareness is awakened while the body is asleep, it can extend far beyond the confines of the physical body and have out-of-body experiences. You are not a body in which awareness comes and goes but rather awareness in a body that comes and goes.

Dr. LaBerge discovered that lucid dreaming is a learnable skill. He has proven by scientific method in a laboratory setting that prearranged signals coming from someone who is dreaming can be measured using the mind-body connection. For example, a sleeping lucid dreamer can look left and then right on a previously arranged cue and those eye movements can be recorded by an observer.

To engage in lucid dreaming, you first need to notice you are dreaming. Occasionally, this realization is triggered by the dreamer recognizing something impossible in the dream, like flying or meeting someone who has died, but most often it is a learned skill.

The idea of waking in the asleep dream has been sought after as a door to awareness and enlightenment for centuries. The Toltec, like many others, had a lucid dreaming practice. They would train themselves to awaken in the dream by looking at their hands and asking, *Am I dreaming?* Looking at their hands over and over while awake was supposed to create a cue to be recognized in the asleep dream. The hope was that one night while dreaming, a lucid dreamer would look at his or her hands and have the magical thought, *Am I dreaming?*

That particular thought in the asleep dream takes an enormous amount of energy. Noticing that you are dreaming while you are asleep is a breakthrough—a stupendous leap of awareness. To make that leap, the Toltec devised a powerful process to help one navigate from unconscious dreaming to lucid dreaming—the Gates of Lucid Dreaming.

The Gates of Lucid Dreaming

The first gate of lucid dreaming is being able to remember your dreams. This step is about having an intention, a thought in mind, to honor and recognize your dreaming world. Keeping a notebook by your bed and being willing to get up and write down your dreams in the middle of the night indicate that you are open to examining your dreams. As simple as it seems, this is a powerful step. Until we make the decision to take the journey, until we take action, not much is going to happen.

Knowing you are dreaming opens the second gate of lucid dreaming. This takes focus and determination, enough to shake off the routine of only remembering your dreams when you get up in the morning. Walking through the second gate is a flawless act of awareness in the very moment of dreaming.

The third gate of lucid dreaming opens when you can use your will to make conscious choices in your dream. This final gate is reached when you can pay attention, ask questions, travel, and take some control of your dream.

Many people arrive at the second gate of dreaming (knowing you are dreaming), lose focus, and lapse into a familiar habit, like being busy and multitasking, then fall back into unconscious dreaming. Others arrive at the second gate of dreaming, get excited, and immediately wake up. That's because their reason tries to take over. They have exquisite feelings, and then the mind chimes in and the feelings evaporate. Recognizing that you are dreaming frequently sets off the habit of needing to define things, having an opinion about what is going on, focusing in, and asking why. Needing to create a definition for everything you are experiencing wakes the language mind, immediately pulls you out of dreaming, and keeps the third gate hopelessly out of reach.

Waking up in your asleep dream to experience lucid dreaming is vastly entertaining and can be highly pleasurable. Lucid dreaming can be used as a rehearsal for life, problem solving, overcoming nightmares, and even healing the physical body. But the real benefit of learning lucid dreaming is to apply it to the other half of your dreaming life, the awake life-dream. The mind is always dreaming, asleep or awake. To notice how amazing belief is and how it affects everything we experience takes pure cognition—the focus of your awareness that is not impaired by the relentlessness of thought.

Being aware in your everyday waking dream is *lucid living*. Lucid living is directly experiencing the dreamlike nature of your personal virtual reality in this present moment. If you want to engage in lucid living and begin to put belief to work, it is enormously helpful to use the pattern presented by the gates of lucid dreaming: the passage from unconscious dreaming to conscious dreaming.

The First Gate of Lucid Living

To begin to practice lucid living, start with the model presented in the first gate of lucid dreaming. Have the intention to recognize your dreaming world. If you want to see life without the overlay of the interpreter who lives in your head and the unseen filter of everything you believe, you first need to state your desire to do so. You have to decide you're interested and take action to express that interest. Lao Tzu, the ancient Chinese philosopher, gives this simple advice: Even a journey of a thousand miles begins with a single step.

In order to be aware of your waking life-dream (what goes on all day in your virtual world as a reaction to what happens inside and outside of you) carry a notebook and write down what you notice. And don't make it personal. Be an impartial reporter. Whatever you write down about yourself or others, do it without judgment. Don't be critical or label things as good or bad. Just observe and keep an inventory of what you experience.

The Second Gate of Lucid Living

This gate is opened when you begin to recognize that the virtual image you see in your mind is constantly being filtered, interpreted, and modified by what you believe. Opening this gate requires two things—using your energy impeccably and developing a cue.

To arrive at the second gate of lucid living takes energy. How do you get more energy? It's simple. Stop wasting it.

We often spend our personal allotment of daily energy in a myriad of ways that don't serve us: poor habits that tax the physical body; assuming we know what's going on and distorting what is said; taking things personally; having a favorite flavor of emotional drama or getting caught up in others' little dramas; choosing situations that result in chronic stress; gossiping; tolerating things we can change; being convinced that somehow everything is about us; indulging in complaining or acting like a victim.

All these things can add up to physical and emotional turmoil that affects us like being pursued by one of Harry Potter's Dementors, dark-hooded creatures who have the ability to suck the life and happiness out of those around them.

If you want to conserve your energy, pay attention to how you use your energy.

- *How easily do you get frustrated?*
- *Do you have a habit of assuming things?*
- *What happens when your expectations aren't being met?*
- *Do you gossip about others and have an opinion about how they should act?*
- *Do you grab at past experiences and predict what will happen next?*

Watch how you use your words, with yourself and those around you.

- *What are you creating by what you say?*
- *Do you have a phrase or expression that you use frequently? What does it say about you?*
- *Do you inject your opinion or experiences into every conversation you have?*
- *Are you addicted to a certain flavor of emotional reaction?*

Examining these questions in your day-to-day living can begin to give you an awareness of how you may be expending excess energy through needless conversation and emotional flare-ups. When you spend your energy unnecessarily, you dilute your ability to see things as they really are.

Another useful device for passing through the second gate of lucid living is developing a cue. A cue is simply a signal, reminder, hint, or suggestion. The Toltec devised the cue to look at their hands, but make one up if you like. Any cue will do. You will need a cue to remind yourself to challenge the truth of what you're experiencing in any moment. When you remember the cue, ask:

Wait a minute . . . what is going on right now? What am I dreaming?

Remembering the cue triggers a different point of view. Rather than being stuck in reaction, blaming others, or blindly assuming things are the way you think they are, ask yourself questions that trigger disbelief. Be a skeptic and don't automatically accept that what you are convinced you are experiencing is completely true.

Are you absolutely sure you know exactly who you are, and what is really going on right now?

You are boundless awareness witnessing itself as a

particular person in time. You are both the source of today's life-dream and a character in it. You are experiencing life from a particular point of view—one that is always changing. Think back ten years. How much of what you were so sure about is true for you today? Who you are today may not be who you are tomorrow. What you are right now is your identity. But that changes. Your identity today is not who you are, but rather who you temporarily appear to be.

So, especially in moments of stress or emotional reaction, stop, take a breath, do an internal inventory, and ask yourself questions that support disbelief. Questions like:

- *What's happening with me?* (Focus inside yourself rather than making it about others.)
- *How do I feel?*
- *What is the voice in my mind telling me? Is it true? Is it absolutely true?*

Look at yourself in the mirror. What do you see in your face? Take an inventory of how you are feeling in your body. How is your body posture? Are you relaxed? Tense? Is your breathing deep and full, or short and shallow?

Having the presence of mind to remember to notice these things when life veers off in an unexpected direction is more powerful than you can imagine. It takes energy, perhaps more than you have right now, to recall the cue in the middle of the whirlwind that is everyday life.

It takes gathering your energy and recovering your attention to be able to observe what you are dreaming while you are awake.

Your attention (the focus of your awareness) is normally captivated by the voice of the interpreter telling you all about what you believe. Recovering your attention allows you to notice so much more than what is usually going on within the narrow confines of the Island of the Known. Gathering your energy and remembering to ask questions that spur disbelief allow you to develop your attention—your life-dream attention. Passing through the second gate of lucid living and noticing your unique life-dream instantly creates expanded perception.

The Third Gate of Lucid Living

Making conscious choices and decisions with the awareness that your beliefs modify your awake-dream will bring you to the third gate of lucid living. You'll approach this gate when you decide to honor the intuitive part of your awareness, make a real attempt to conserve your energy, and accept your own accountability as the creator of the dream. It's your dream!

Moving with authority in the dream of your life happens when you recognize that there is an engine driving your actions, you are living your dream, and you construct your own interpretation of reality simply by what you agree to believe.

Two things are very helpful in opening the third gate of lucid living: *Stop the World* and *Give Up the Need to Be Right.*

Stop the World is a simple practice for letting your description of how things appear to be collapse for a few minutes each day. It is much like mindfulness or meditation, but more. Meditation is now practiced every week by more than ten million people in the United States alone, and taught in schools, corporate settings, hospitals, and prisons. The payoffs of meditating include stress reduction, enhanced memory, and relief from insomnia, high blood pressure, anxiety, and depression. (An exercise describing "Stop the World" can be found on pages 159–160.)

Meditation is an ancient practice, but in the modern world it is often sold using the obvious benefits along with catchy names, trademarked modalities, and secret mantras. Stripped of all the window dressing, the intent is simple and straightforward. *Stop the world*, your private world, so that you can witness what is—right now—without the overlay of what you think it is always hooking your attention. Stopping the world, noticing life without the dominance of the language mind and exercising the dreaming mind, is an essential skill that throws open the third gate of lucid living.

A lot of people have trouble practicing mindfulness because they approach it as a way to suppress the language mind. *Sit still and stop your thoughts!* I prefer using it as a way to fulfill my desire.

Imagine your favorite dessert. Close your eyes. In your dreaming mind, smell it, taste it, and feel the texture rolling off your tongue.

Perhaps through this little exercise you have conjured up the feeling and desire you have when you are about to enjoy a treat you adore. What you have done is create a point of view, a little dream, in no time at all. Stopping the World is also a little dream. It's an inner place of relaxation, a quiet presence in the undulating eternal now. If you know how it feels, if you have a reference point, you can go there in an instant, propelled by your desire—with your eyes closed or *with your eyes open*.

Another step that will allow you to instantly pass through the third gate of lucid living is giving up the need to be right. Needing to be right is a way to create safety and fortify the island of what you know. Being right defends, justifies, and protects your assumptions, attachments, expectations, and opinions—your entire personal story with all its hard-earned knowledge.

Michael had a doctorate from an Ivy League university and was on his way to being a tenured professor. He had a conflict he was trying to work out with a colleague, a woman researcher who also worked at the university. As soon as he walked in the door, he apologized for coming to see me because, as he explained, he normally could solve any problem he was having on his own. Once he sat down, he relaxed a bit and told me every little detail about his conflict with his colleague, having examined it from all possible angles.

Every time I tried to offer a question or different viewpoint to consider, he interrupted me. His response to everything I tried to suggest was, "Yes, but . . ."

"Michael," I finally said, "There is nothing I can do for you."

"Why?"

"Because you're always right!"

There was no way I could help him. The "Yes, but . . ." said it all. Michael was addicted to being right.

Passing through the third gate of lucid living is a journey into the unknown. As valuable as all the experience and knowledge you've accumulated might be, when you're right you are only going to see what you know. You learn very little when you insist on being right. What you notice may be accurate, but being right is a judgment, an assessment that distorts everything you perceive. Being right opens a narrow bandwidth of perception and nothing more. To approach the third gate of lucid living demands a different attitude—the humble, open posture of *I don't know*. Deliberately choosing *I don't know* when approaching the third gate of lucid living is not a sign of weakness. It's an act of power.

If you want to harness the power of belief, you will have to use both sides of your awareness because that's how beliefs are built in the first place. You fabricated your beliefs by using all your tools of perception, opening a channel of communication, agreeing, collecting evidence, and over a long period of time, investing your faith in a particular point of view. You create your personal life-dream using not only your language mind, but your dreaming mind as well. Past the words, the reason, the things in life that are solid and unchanging lies the unseen part of life that is fluid, mysterious, and sometimes overwhelming. Unseating the ruler of the language mind, the chatter of the mitote, and taking the steps to open true awareness—*perception without judgment*—throws open the gates of lucid living. Practicing lucid living cultivates clarity, puts you in charge of your BeliefWorks, and engages the totality of your human being—body, mind, and spirit.

Part Two

Your Intent Is a Force

What is essential is invisible to the eye.

—*Antoine de Saint-Exupéry*

The Four Elements of Belief

EVERY MOMENT OF YOUR LIFE IS SO STRONGLY INFLUENCED by what you believe that changing any belief that is an obstacle to accomplishing what you desire is like alchemy.

Alchemy, a practice with origins as far back in time as ancient Egypt, was the quest to change base metals into gold. To accomplish this, alchemists proposed using the Philosopher's Stone, a mysterious substance they believed to have the power to transmute lead—a dull, dense, and common element—into gold, a glittering precious commodity. But transforming lead into gold to obtain riches was a ruse used to protect the powers of the Philosopher's Stone. True alchemy wasn't concerned with upgrading less valuable metals, but rather with healing the human body and spirit. The Philosopher's Stone was a magical substance thought to cure illness, prolong life, bring about personal growth, and—at the height of its powers—lead to spiritual enlightenment.

The core idea of alchemy is allegorical, an extended metaphor full of beautiful symbolism. Its underlying philosophy is the same as BeliefWorks: that we can take the dull and sometimes confining reality we have created as a result of our personal agreements and transform it into something precious simply by recrafting the beliefs that limit us.

The construction of belief is a holistic process—a process encompassing the *whole* human being. Belief is not just about what you think is true, nor is belief changed simply by changing your mind. Your entire system of belief was assembled by using your language mind, your dreaming mind, and all your tools of perception, cemented together by the investment of your faith.

Belief is the product of all our experiences and our decisions about those experiences. Over time, we construct a matrix of beliefs that invades our dreams, awake or asleep, creating a virtual reality that sometimes resembles gold—glittering and precious—and that in other moments acts like lead—heavy and seemingly unchangeable.

In either case, to tune up your BeliefWorks so that it produces the dream of life you desire may require a little alchemy on the four essential elements of belief.

Air—The First Element of Belief

The ancient alchemists believed there were four base elements from which everything was made—Air, Water, Fire, and Earth.

Air symbolizes our mental faculties and ability to perceive. The element of Air has two distinct parts that create the whole—*perception* and *intellect.*

PERCEPTION is an ingredient of the dreaming mind, the part of you that is aware and notices without words. You perceive your surroundings through the physical senses of sight, taste, touch, hearing, and smell, as well as the nonphysical: emotion and the focus of your awareness, your attention.

As you collect information, a biochemical process in your brain creates a virtual image from all the sensory input you accumulate. For example, light reflecting off any object in front of you strikes the retina in your eye and, through a series of electrical and chemical reactions, creates an image in your mind. You perceive the world through your tools of perception and continually construct a personal life-dream modified by your own unique filter of beliefs.

Our tools of perception translate energy, intuition, and physical sensation into the biochemical and electrical processes that allow us to sense the world. We are always perceiving both the physical world and things seemingly outside of the physical realm, whether we are aware or not. From the standpoint of science, things in the physical world can be measured. By nonphysical, I mean what is experienced and seems to be real, yet cannot be measured except for its effect on the physical body. A good example is the emotions we feel.

There are so many instances of nonphysical perception. Have you ever been waiting for someone in a crowded place, and you knew exactly when they arrived without even looking? Many people report that when someone close to them was hurt or died, they felt something was wrong long before they received the actual news. Synchronicity is another example. Have you ever been thinking about someone and he or she called you on the phone or you met unexpectedly?

Most of the time, however, we have too much on our minds to notice the world of nonphysical perception.

In late December 2004, an earthquake measuring 9.0

on the Richter scale cracked open the seabed off
Indonesia's Sumatra Island. What followed was a giant
tsunami causing a great loss of life, not only in the beach
communities near the epicenter of the earthquake, but
also in coastal villages up to 1,500 miles away.

One video, shot by a tourist standing on the balcony
of his hotel, showed a massive wave crashing through the
trees at the edge of a resort beach while a small group of
people a hundred yards inland were standing around the
pool, chatting and sipping their beverages, completely
unaware of what was about to happen.

Despite the enormous number of human casualties,
there were very few reports of animals caught by the tor-
rent of the tsunami. In Sri Lanka's national wildlife park
at Yala—which houses elephants, buffalo, monkeys, and
wild cats—no animal bodies were found, yet only 30 of
the 250 tourist vehicles that entered the park that day
returned to base.

In Khao Lak, Thailand, elephants trained to give people rides began to cry and trumpet that day and could
not be comforted by their handlers. They ran with
tourists aboard up the jungle-clad hill behind the resort
beach just before the tsunami arrived.

On the day of the tsunami, many animals sensed that
trouble was on the way. History is littered with tales of
creatures acting oddly before natural disasters, but the
phenomenon has been hard for science to pin down.
Animals do not have the human capacity to reason, but
their physical senses are acute and, like us, they feel.
Their feelings are intelligent, carrying simple messages
like *food, danger,* and *safe.* Measurable or not, a percepti-
ble force moves ahead of an event like a tsunami and animals seem to sense it.

What we notice with our physical senses, what is

apparent based on what we know from previous experience, is frequently only a portion of what is. What is unseen below the surface is sometimes more significant than what is seen. In Hawaii, banyan trees have root systems that are more massive than the tree that grows above ground. Three quarters of an iceberg floating in the Arctic Circle lies hidden underneath the surface of the water. What we think we are aware of, our intellectual realizations and obvious physical sensations, are often not the whole, but only the tip of the iceberg.

INTELLECT is our ability to analyze what we perceive. We take what is collected through perception and apply reason. We organize information, examine the data, ask questions, formulate agreements, and develop arguments about what point of view is valid. From those arguments we generate opinions about how things are. And finally we make decisions. Based on our opinions, we choose what to do.

Intellect is a component of the language mind, the part that thinks and reasons with words. Sometimes the balance between perception (the dreaming mind) and intellect (the language mind) is lost and our reason and the words it speaks take control.

Your earliest awareness of the world (the First Dream) occured when adults captured your attention, taught you language, opened a channel of communication, and told you about everything they knew. This process of capturing your attention for the first time creates, by agreement, your initial life-dream of how the world is.

As adults teach us their interpretation of perception, the sounds and concepts that make up language, they open channels of communication into their own personal reality. Before we learned language, we operated with the intelligence of what we felt and perceived largely without judgment, like the animals at Yala. In the construction of the First Dream we develop a thinking mind filled with words. If the adults around us are weighted by their intellect and let their dreaming mind wither, we become domesticated in the very same way. We lose the ability to notice the essence of the present moment and let ourselves be dominated by the intellect and its narrow gaze. Over time, each opinion, each idea, each concept we face makes an impression, but only if we agree. And if some of these opinions are laced with unreasonable fear, they become a virus in the structure of our thoughts. At a certain point most of us become overpowered by a runaway mind, a mind with many voices talking at once, an intellect that runs the show, a mitote—a voice of knowledge filled with many fear-based judgments that now rules our attention.

The alchemy of Air is simply to put everything back in balance, to restore the perfect counterpoint of intellect and perception. To renew the equilibrium of Air is to understand that awareness operates in concert with reason and the power of language. Nonstop speech or an inner dialog careening out of control driven by unfounded fears must be uncovered and cleaned before balance can be restored.

Try this exercise. Decide for one day to take a vow of silence. Speak only when it is essential, and say only what is required. What do you notice? Is what you are thinking about all the time really necessary? Are all the words you speak during a day the very best use of your energy?

The alchemy of Air is achieved by practicing mindfulness and silence—stopping the world—balanced by applying your intellect as a tool, a power tool brought out only when it's required for the job at hand.

Water—The Second Element of Belief

To the alchemists, the element of Water signified our emotional nature. The element of Water also has two distinct parts: *emotion in the moment* and *emotion in memory*.

Your emotions are a membrane through which you perceive the world. In the same way the five physical senses send impulses to the brain that are translated into sensory perception, emotions translate your intuition and instant insights into feelings. Emotion is an essential component of your integrity. Emotions are always full of good information because they never, ever lie.

**Even without words—without
definition or description—emotions
provide guidance and essential information
translating intuition into feelings.**

EMOTION IN THE MOMENT is the intelligent response from our membrane of feeling, full of key information, that is always telling us the truth.

Suppose you go for a hike in the mountains, come around the corner, and suddenly find yourself standing at the precipice of a thousand-foot cliff. Before you have a chance to think about where you are, there is an emotional response—real fear. Your immediate reaction is to move away from the edge of the cliff. The emotion provides perfect guidance before you have time to think.

Emotions provide wordless direction and important information. I've had many people tell me they were taught it's not okay to show emotions or trust them. But when we ignore or go against our emotional intelligence we threaten our basic health and happiness.

An example: Soldiers returning from war sometimes suffer from post-traumatic stress disorder (PTSD). Faced with the horrors of war, they ignore the fear they experience because of the agreements of duty. Soldiers are forced to endure the situation they are in regardless of the intense emotional messages they get. They stuff their feelings and just keep going. Once they are back in normal circumstances, soldiers suffering from PTSD exhibit symptoms such as sleeplessness, frequent agitation, shallow breathing, constipation, and an accelerated heart rate. They have nightmares, flashbacks, anxiety, unreasonable fear, and uncontrollable emotional outbursts. Intimacy on every level is impossible. War-related PTSD teaches the lesson that when the intelligence of the emotional messages in the moment is repeatedly ignored, the result is frequently long-term damage to our human being.

Tom was a 19-year-old from Missoula, Montana, when he enlisted in the Marines. Six months later he was sent to fight in the Vietnam War. "My job," he recalled, "was to kill and orchestrate the killing. I had been living by a moral code, a code of virtue. I was taught that they were wrong and we were right. My use of this moral code led me astray and caused me great pain. I'm not a sociopath or person who doesn't care. After I got back home, I wondered—how could I do this? What I discovered through years of guilt and shame is I am intrinsically moral. My whole being told me in those situations exactly what to do. My body balked and felt sick when I was confronted with what I was told I was *supposed* to do."

Have you ever heard someone say, "I knew it was wrong but I did it anyway"? At one time or another, I think we all do that and later find it difficult to forgive ourselves. Every society all over the world has codes of conduct taught by parents, the law, and religion. Yet these codes can be corrupted in so many ways, producing guilt, shame, or pain. In some situations it's even virtuous to feel guilt, shame, or pain! Beyond all the confusing signals, I think this is simple. Every one of us has a built-in moral compass—emotion. Perhaps we ignore it, or do the thing that causes harm anyway, but it is always there. My body and my in-the-moment emotions have always told me exactly what to do regardless of what I was possessed by, thinking, or was *supposed* to do.

EMOTION IN MEMORY is the emotional point of view of a past pivotal experience. When the event happened, the emotion associated with your experience was telling you the truth. If that memory is triggered by something in this moment, the emotion that arises is often full of lies.

A pattern of similar incidents repeated again and again eventually becomes belief—a distinct point of view with a series of agreements about what happened that define and defend that point of view. On rare occasions, an overwhelming and riveting incident—like an accident, stroke of amazing luck, or tragedy—results in a new belief. Either way, every experience, every incident has an emotional perspective to it. Not only do beliefs contain memory, pictures, intent, and dialog, but beliefs created over time by reinforcement and repetition have an emotional point of view. The lens of belief that filters your virtual reality always contains emotions in memory.

The stories that emanate from your beliefs always have an emotional point of view.

Anna's uncle came to live with her family when she was ten years old. He had just broken up with his wife, was surly and sarcastic, and whispered mean things under his breath. None of the kids felt safe while he was around. Late one night, he came home drunk and there was a loud argument between her mother, father, and her uncle. All the kids hid under their beds until it was over and to everyone's relief he moved out the next day.

Now, 30 years later, Anna is noticeably agitated by loud disagreements. She will do *anything* to diffuse the situation, make everyone happy, and restore peace.

The emotion that comes up when there is any sort of commotion is strangely familiar for Anna. It's the emotional perspective of a ten-year-old girl hiding under the bed. When her uncle lived with the family, the emotion she felt was full of good information. There was an unhappy man with a dream full of fear living in her house. Her emotion identified his outbursts for what they were: *Not-Love.* The emotional response to not-love is authentic and very informative. Not-love doesn't feel good, and in the dream of a child it doesn't feel safe. Today, for Anna, the emotional memory that rises in any vaguely similar situation is full of lies—things that were true then but are not necessarily true about what is happening right now.

The alchemy of Water occurs when we learn to honor this extraordinary part of who we are. Every moment has an emotional signature and so the built-in perception of emotion deserves our complete attention and total respect.

What would happen if the next time you are overwhelmed by strong emotion, you let the emotion be just as it is and resist the impulse to explain it, run from it, or fix it?

When we get triggered and an unpleasant emotion arises, it ignites a story that goes hand in hand with the flavor of the emotion. Sometimes we escalate the drama by arguing, assuming, being right, defending, or blaming. Or perhaps we do anything we can to avoid feeling at all.

The next time you feel overwhelmed by an emotion, let it inform you about the viewpoint of what you are feeling. Ask yourself:

Is this the authentic emotional perspective of what is happening in this moment, or a familiar pattern released by an emotion in my memory?

The emotional messages we receive are valuable guideposts to potent action, and awareness of emotion in memory is essential to healing long-forgotten limiting agreements.

Fire—The Third Element of Belief

To the alchemists, Fire symbolized our pursuit of purpose. Not a singular purpose, but the movement to action. What drives us to act, to do something, is the force of Life. As always, this element has two complementary parts, one that resides in the language mind and the other in the dreaming mind. The element of Fire is made up of *intention* and *intent*.

INTENTION, the first component of Fire, is the intellectual portion of action. What you intend to do is what you have "in mind." Intention is your mental agreement about how to proceed, a determination propelling you toward some action, some purpose in the moment.

Intention manifests from your language mind. If it is occupied by a program, your filter of belief, then your actions will be driven by all the agreements you've made with yourself about who you are and what the world is. If any of those agreements were born out of fear, there is a virus in the program and all your wishing, wanting, and hoping are no more than an impassioned flight from that fear. In fact, the essence of that fear will be your intention.

An example: Let's say you start a business. You want to have fun, be successful, and grow the business into something that gives you financial security far into the future. One morning, sitting in the kitchen eating breakfast, you read a newspaper article that says more than 70 percent of all new businesses fail within the first two years. After reading the article you begin to worry. Perhaps your business isn't growing as fast as you thought it would. Every time things don't go the way you want them to, you keep replaying in your mind the story from the article. Pretty soon whatever is driving your decisions is directly coupled to the fear of failing. At that point, what you are worried about has become your intention.

INTENT, the second component of Fire, is an active force applied through your attention, the focus of your awareness. Life uses the force of intent to manifest itself. You use the force of intent to manifest your own life, which includes assembling all of your beliefs.

Intent is not a mental decision, yet it is initiated by a

mental decision—your intention. If intention is *what you have in mind,* intent is *what you mean to do.* Describing intent is like trying to describe how you feel. Intent is directed life force, changing moment to moment. Intent is not wishing or hoping; it is knowing with absolute faith.

When you focus your intent, once there is a choice, you invoke a force that makes things happen. Every act of creation is intent followed by action.

**Your intent moves by faith and invokes
the attention and intent of Life itself.**

My first real understanding of intent came while I was studying aikido. Aikido is a modern defensive Japanese martial art derived from judo and the Samurai sword arts.

One spring I took a class with a sensei (teacher) who had an exercise where she would blindfold the student, put him in the middle of the room, and instruct him to move, defending himself in the direction of his attacker. When it was my turn, I was blindfolded and had my hearing muffled. She led me into the middle of the mat and touched my arm as a signal to begin. I couldn't see or hear my attacker, and so the only action possible was to move and put my arms up when I sensed something coming toward me.

After a few weeks of practicing I got pretty good at it. And something odd began to happen.

Each night I would walk my dog through the neighborhood to exercise her. Over and over as I was walking her I would feel something, and without thinking about it, turn toward the feeling. At first there was nothing there, and then suddenly someone would open the door to their house, or a car would come around the corner, or an animal would appear in the shadows. I began to notice with some regularity a feeling signaling a moving force always preceding someone or something in action.

The alchemy of Fire is accomplished simply by noticing what you focus on and throttling back the engine of fear. When you recognize the interplay between intention (what you have in mind) and intent (the force of Life you use to make things happen) one thing becomes very clear: You set into motion whatever you believe is true.

Earth—The Fourth Element of Belief

The final element of belief is represented by Earth. The Earth is an immense bio-system contained in space by the mysterious force of gravity. *Gaia,* as the ancient Greeks called Earth 3,000 years ago, is the mother of nature—a living being. Many native cultures around the world today still consider the Earth to be a conscious being—a living thing that dreams.

The essence of the final element of belief, Earth, is the power to manifest, through consciousness and dreaming, an entire universe of reality.

The essence of the final element of belief is the power to manifest. The power to create reality. The power to dream.

Like all the other elements, the element of Earth has two distinct parts that create the whole: *the dreamer* and *the dream.*

The human mind is alive and one of its main purposes is to dream. From that dreaming we create a unique virtual reality that lives inside our heads, a private universe that supports whatever we believe. When the element of Earth is out of balance, the personal dream created over time begins to dream the dreamer. We are so wrapped up in all the little day-to-day details of our life-dream that we really don't notice what we are dreaming. We think we know what is going on but we don't. We unconsciously interpret life rather than experiencing it. We forget our old agreements, and our beliefs invisibly begin to run every part of our lives.

Our power to dream is full of possibility, bursting with potential. When we lose awareness of that power, we still use it, but our BeliefWorks runs unnoticed in the background, often in a way that doesn't serve our best or highest interests.

You are a complex matrix of matter, thought, emotion, and energy. You are one-awareness, a witnessing presence in body, a life-dreamer experiencing life from a particular point of view. The alchemy of Earth occurs when you, the dreamer, recognize the power of your dreaming and consciously use awareness to direct the extraordinary forces of belief.

When you balance the four elements of belief—Air: intellect and perception; Water: emotion in the moment and emotion in memory; Fire: intention and intent; and Earth: the dream and the dreamer—all the potential of belief is within reach. Skillfully engage the four elements of belief and the miraculous mystery of life will become your ever-changing, carefully crafted masterpiece!

A Marriage of Opposites

GENE NATHAN IS A PEDIATRICIAN IN SAN DIEGO, California. He has been a family doctor for almost 30 years. What he's seen over the last few years troubles him deeply.

"I used to treat children for chronic headaches a few times a year. Now I see four or five kids a week who have persistent headaches. I think the numbers are increasing because they're stressed by too much doing," says Dr. Gene, as he likes to be called.

"A lot of parents don't allow their kids to just be kids. They want their children to experience as much as possible, and the world is moving too fast for them. They're on overload, running from here to there in a mad dash until the family members go to their respective screens at the end of the day. If kids aren't in front of a computer or a television, they're watching life sped up from the back of a car."

Dr. Gene continues, "We see more sports injuries than when I started out in practice. When children play naturally and a muscle gets stressed, they do something else. Now they hardly get to play at all. Too many kids are experiencing a constant demand for performance. They're at school all day and then go straight to organized sports. Parents who run these programs stress competition that's supposed to prepare kids for an adult world. Little kids playing soccer are being sized up with statistics fed into the coach's laptop computer. And then the kids go even faster because they think play should be *extreme* like they see on TV. It's way too much."

For children and adults alike, the world is speeding up. The digital revolution has made it possible to get mail, do business, buy products, and play games instantaneously with millions of other people almost anywhere on the planet. Global communication and personal electronic technology hold the tantalizing promise of helping us do more in less time. But the relentless pursuit of growth, efficiency, and accomplishment is quickly taking its toll on our most basic sense of well-being.

The pulse of life is accelerating. Rather than listen to the whisper of their innermost guidance to find balance, many people get a pill, gulp it down, and keep on going.

Some examples: Over the past ten years worldwide sales of serotonin-enhancing antidepressants such as Prozac, Paxil, and Zoloft have exploded. Paxil, the best-selling drug of the three, is used to treat more than 59 million patients (including 11 million children) each year. These families of drugs are prescribed for the treatment of depression that interferes with daily functioning, obsession, and compulsion (an obsession is a thought that won't go away; a compulsion is an action done over and over to relieve anxiety). These drugs are also used to treat panic disorders (feelings of intense fear that develop suddenly, often for no reason). This revolution in biological psychiatry is frequently the solution of choice for overwhelmed adults and children alike.

Designed to treat impotence, Viagra is one of the best-selling drugs on the planet. Millions of men all over the world take the drug on a regular basis. Viagra *overrides* the major causes of impotence: fear of intimacy, stress, overwork, depression, poor health habits, and partner conflicts. Viagra and other copycat drugs allow the user to ignore (at least for the moment) the real reason why the ability to get an erection, a normal and natural occurrence in the male human animal, has begun to shut down.

Many people are convinced they need to perform or they will be left behind, and the enormous growth of caffeine consumption is a telling indicator. Caffeine is now every generation's drug of choice, gearing them up for what needs to be done whether they want to do it or not. Energy drinks containing large doses of caffeine and herbal stimulants like ephedrine, guarana, and ginseng have overtaken bottled water as the fastest-growing sellers in the beverage business. The Starbucks Corporation, which sells coffee drinks, started as a local coffee shop in Pike Place Market on the waterfront in Seattle, Washington. Just 13 years after going public, it has more than 6,300 locations in 30 countries (yes, there is one on every other corner!) with annual revenues of $5.6 billion and climbing. Next to military arms and oil, coffee is the largest commodity-based industry in the world; except for water, it is the most popular drink on the planet.

The world is quickening and in order to keep up, we are hooked on the idea of doing more, doing it faster, and achieving all that we can. We are told by every corner of the media that the ultimate in being healthy is to operate at full throttle, feeling alive and connected to life. Even the idea of harvesting the force of belief seems to be on the same track—communicate effectively, create consciously, and gain personal power through action. But looking closer, it's not. Nonstop doing is out of balance, ignores the signs that undermine wellness, and runs on a track of fear.

Not-Doing

The Toltec had an interesting device they called *not-doing*. Not-doing does not mean doing nothing. Not-doing is a decision you make to consider the opposite of what you have always been doing, because that point of view may be worth exploring. Not-doing is about suspending judgment, dropping what you are so sure you are right about, and stepping off the island of what you know to get a better view.

All of us are guilty, at one time or another, of going through life half-asleep with blinders on, propelled by the engine of fear, unaware of our agreements, or caught up in habits born out of someone else's fear: habits such as saying yes when we mean no, feeling obligated to act according to someone else's wishes, staying at a job that holds no promise, or not having the courage to move on in a relationship when it's over.

Not-doing is simply the act of suspending habitual unconscious doing for the purpose of fostering awareness and regaining your balance. Nonstop doing is driven by the language mind. Not-doing is a perspective fostered by your dreaming mind.

In the doing of daily life we are like this and like that. We operate exclusively on the island of what we know. What is, and what we are capable of, are neatly contained within our description of how things are. This description is held together because we defend it, nurture it, and insist we are right, even if it doesn't feel good.

Belief, however, is holistic and contains elements far outside the narrow path carved by rational thought and nonstop action. To harvest the force of belief involves developing the dreaming mind in equal balance with the language mind. Our human being is nourished by balance, never by the imbalance caused by nonstop doing.

Not-doing opens possibilities that exist only outside the island of what you know. Engaging in not-doing considers viewpoints that embrace the opposite of your normal doing as equal and valid complements to what you normally do.

Not-doing requires that you not accept as absolute truth all the things you think or say. The next time you feel stressed or react emotionally, listen very carefully to the dialog in your own mind. Is what you are saying to defend your point of view true? Is it *really* true? Just that little bit of doubt opens another way of looking at things that has very little to do with the intellect. Faith holds your beliefs together and absence of faith will crack them open. That's not-doing.

Isaac, the man whose father died of a brain tumor when he was 13, created a universe of his own making and endured 40 years of pain because of it. He seemed to be hopelessly stuck, with no way out. That was his pattern of *doing*. I suggested not-doing, abandoning the viewpoint that he had nurtured for so long. Taking my suggestion, he decided to give up needing to be right about what happened. He gave up defending his interpretation with no solution other than not-doing. Not-doing gave him access to another point of view with a completely different emotional signature and set of agreements. When he experienced that life-dream, for only a moment, everything changed.

A Marriage of Opposites

In ancient China, the keeper of the Imperial Library, Lao Tzu, was famous for his wisdom. Perceiving growing corruption within the government, he decided to leave for the countryside. According to legend, as Lao Tzu was on his way out of the city gates, a guard asked him to write about the essence of his understanding of life to benefit future generations. Lao Tzu wrote the *Tao Te Ching*, or "How Things Work," and was never heard from again.

The *Tao Te Ching* is one of the most influential books in history. The philosophy of the Tao is represented by a circular symbol. Inside of the circle are two intertwining teardrop shapes, one black and one white. The black teardrop, Yin, signifies the characteristics of the moon, the direction north, softness, and receptivity. The original meaning of Yin is "the north side of the hill—away from the sun." Yin represents feminine nature. The white teardrop, Yang, signifies the characteristics of the sun, the direction south, activity, hardness, and brightness. The original meaning of Yang is "the south side of the hill—facing the sun." Yang represents masculine nature.

The symbol of the Tao shows two opposing forces in a circular dance with no beginning or end. They revolve around one another, alternating in a continuous cycle.

Where one is at its maximum, the other is at its minimum. Inside the largest part of the dark area is a light spot, and inside the largest part of the light area is a dark spot, as if the seed of one is always living and growing in the greatest expression of the other.

The symbol of the Tao is a wonderful representation of how things are in the natural world. It also illustrates the wedding of doing and not-doing, a marriage of opposites.

We exist in an ever-revolving series of opposing forces, the heartbeat of life. Sun and moon. Low tide and high tide. Winter and summer. We breathe in and we breathe out.

Business and economies are cyclical, rising and falling. Despite the unwavering demand in business for growth and greater profits, the development of ideas and products demands reflection—an inward process of research and inquiry—and then to make it happen, action.

**Everything that is in balance embraces
not-doing and the marriage of opposites.**

Perhaps the reason you are interested in harnessing the power of belief is to grow, do better, and evolve toward your goals, hopes, and dreams. But that is doing on top of doing. And the underlying message in nonstop doing is—*it's not enough.* In fact, it will *never* be enough. The fundamental agreement lodged in perpetual doing is: *Everything will be okay when . . .*

Everything will be okay when . . . is a point of view that only focuses on the future and has no perspective of the presence and fullness of Now. The not-doing of *Everything will be okay when . . .* is to embrace and open up in gratitude to Now.

How can I wed two opposing points of view like:
"I want to achieve my greatest dreams"
and
"Everything is okay right now."

At first glance they contradict each other, but that's not really true. How can you join these contrasting attitudes? It's easy.

Breathe in: I choose to grow, face my problems, and evolve.

Breathe out: Everything is perfect in this moment, just as it is.

Breathe in: I am absolutely clear about what I want.

Breathe out: I surrender to the mystery of life.

Breathe in: I deeply desire my vision of the future.

Breathe out: I'm okay in this moment with whatever happens.

Breathe in: I'm passionate and going after what I want.

Breathe out: I release all control and let go.

Although they appear to be completely opposite points of view, they are not.

**You can pursue your dreams and
rest in the perfection of now.**

In balance, we are a marriage, a blending of opposites. The Toltec described all that we are as *the totality of the human being*. This idea is beautifully illustrated by the legend of Quetzalcoatl and Tezcatlipoca.

Quetzalcoatl was the would-be king of the Toltecs. He was a shining spiritual leader, a god of intelligence descended from the Sun, and a Christlike figure to the ancient Meso-American world. Tezcatlipoca, his brother, was a god of mysterious powers originating from the night sky, a wizard appearing frequently as a shape-shifter, trickster, or magician.

As legend has it, Tezcatlipoca was Quetzalcoatl's adversary. He was called *the Smokey Mirror,* the color of black glass obsidian, a volcanic mineral found in and around the ruins of Teotihuacán.

According to the legend, one evening Tezcatlipoca showed Quetzalcoatl his own reflection in the smokey mirror. In the mirror, Quetzalcoatl appeared old, frail, and ugly. Tezcatlipoca convinced Quetzalcoatl to take a few sips of sacred wine, and then to have more, five cups in all. Drunk and feeling sorry for himself, Quetzalcoatl was obsessed with proving he was still vital and powerful. When he awoke the next morning, he discovered he had done many things he was terribly ashamed of. Quetzalcoatl descended into a deep spiral of guilt and remorse, fled to the sea, and sailed into the distance, never to be seen again.

Although this legend suggests these two brothers were enemies, that's not exactly true. One of the many clay masks found in the ancient ruins of Teotihuacán is a three-dimensional sculpture with three faces. Split from forehead to chin, the outer mask is a skull, beneath that is a white face, and underneath the two outer masks is a darker face.

Quetzalcoatl always appears as white, with fair hair. Tezcatlipoca appears as dark-skinned, sometimes as a black jaguar stalking unseen in the darkness of night.

The mask illustrates the idea that Quetzalcoatl and

Tezcatlipoca are actually one person. Together they represent the totality of the human being, the aspects of all that we are. We are tonal—a form in the solid everyday world. We are nagual—the spirit that dreams, awareness inhabiting a human body. In the view of modern physics, we are particles made up of pure energy separated by vast distances of space. In the view of the ancient Toltec we are made of light—both stars and the space between the stars.

The war between Quetzalcoatl and Tezcatlipoca is the war that we sometimes have within ourselves. We are a body, a mind, and awareness that dreams. But when that awareness is overwhelmed by beliefs born of unfounded fears, we create a separate virtual reality that projects itself out into the world. We are convinced that somehow we are not enough. That belief and the emotion it ignites become a destructive force keeping us trapped, robbing us of our energy, and blinding us from truth. The belief, *I'm not enough*, is a fog—a smoke that obscures who we really are. Out of balance and corrupted by fear, Tezcatlipoca is no longer an ally, but a tempter and predator: *the parasite of fear.*

People who practice mindfulness know one thing for sure: When all the words fall away and they rest into the moment, they feel good. Very good. When they allow their worldview to collapse, everything is all right just as it is. What often makes us feel bad is our interpretations, our judgments about what is happening around us and to us.

Doing well and feeling good are not mutually exclusive. They are two portions of the whole. With enough practice, doing and not-doing can happen simultaneously. You can do life, be life, and dream life all at once. There is no conflict. In fact, joining these things together results in greater creativity and well-being— foundations for a whole new set of empowering beliefs.

Embrace the fullness of the power of belief by balancing the intellect with the imagination; the dreaming mind with the language mind; doing along with not-doing, all in a powerful ritual opening up a new universe—a universe beyond what you can begin to imagine—simply by embracing all that you are: an ever-changing marriage of opposites.

Design a New Framework of Agreements

By now almost everyone has heard the story of Enron. At the close of the twentieth century Enron was a corporate jewel in the Houston, Texas, skyline. An energy conglomerate employing more than 21,000 people in more than 40 countries, Enron was the industry leader, growing at a staggering rate—a colossus feeding off new technologies, new markets, and innovation. Like most modern corporations it had a well-formulated mission statement defining its purpose (why the organization exists, what it is going to do, and how it will be done) along with a set of carefully selected core values (principles that guide people's actions and attitudes that uniquely affect an organization's culture).

Enron's stated core values were RICE: *Respect, Integrity, Communication, and Excellence.* This acronym was drummed into employees in a variety of ways. For example, every new hire got a code of ethics booklet at orientation with RICE on the cover. RICE was even emblazoned in large letters on the walls of Enron's massive corporate cafeteria.

By the arrival of spring in 2002, Enron's bankruptcy became the most spectacular corporate collapse in the history of business. As the walls came tumbling down, they revealed the worst of corporate greed, an avalanche triggered by lies and fear. Losses to investors, customers, and employees were shattering—so large that a shudder was felt throughout the global economy. In the aftermath of the collapse, criminal charges were leveled at the firm's top executives. One of the world's most respected accounting companies, Arthur Andersen, with more than 28,000 workers worldwide, was implicated as an accessory and slowly dismantled, accused of accounting fraud.

The conduct of the executives at Enron was hardly an isolated incident. The startling gap between the values an organization proclaims and the actual behavior of its leaders has been exposed many times throughout history, and again in recent criminal proceedings against executives at some of the world's largest corporations.

Criminal indictments and statistics on white-collar crime are not the only yardsticks to measure the disconnect between stated corporate values and what really happens day to day in an organization. All over the world, in thousands of companies both large and small, what is proclaimed as "the way we do business" and what is done in the heat of the moment frequently don't line up.

How does this happen? It is simple to explain. Every action we take is filtered through a matrix of past personal agreements that invisibly overrides what we *think* we *should* do.

There is no way around it: Our reactions and the decisions we make are deeply impacted by the agreements we have made with ourselves that define and defend what we truly believe. This dynamic is exactly the same for individuals as it is for organizations.

If you subscribe to a set of core values and barely address the framework of agreements, personal or collective, that operates powerfully and invisibly below the surface, then those values are no more than a set of empty promises.

Annie and Lee are alcoholics. They met while they were drinking, attended recovery together, fell in love, and eventually married. They religiously attended an alcoholic support group and even lectured for the group in their community, telling their success story as a way to inspire others. Life went well for ten years, and then, seemingly out of the blue, everything went terribly wrong.

Like most couples, Annie and Lee divided their household chores. It was Lee's responsibility to take money out of their joint account and pay the bills. One day, Annie discovered that Lee wasn't paying the credit card bills or the mortgage. She frantically phoned him and left message after message. He didn't answer for three days. When she finally reached him he said, "I can't come back right now." Lee had begun to drink again, was gambling, and had devoured their life savings. Annie eventually filed for divorce.

"He's the love of my life," said Annie, "but I realized that he never changed any of the beliefs that made him an alcoholic in the first place. I did, but he didn't. He traded his addiction to alcohol for another addiction—the rules of recovery. He held on as long as he could and then went right back to it."

**To make a real change, take the time to
discover what beliefs are running the show,
rework those beliefs, and then design agreements
that support the outcome you want.**

When our consulting group is invited into an organization, the first thing we do is find out what beliefs are in force, as well as the agreements that support those beliefs. The core beliefs of the group act like the great and powerful Oz behind the curtain, an invisible undercurrent affecting everything. Once we uncover that, we work through a series of processes to re-script and design new agreements that are in alignment with the organization's desired mission, values, and culture—the dream they have about how they would *like* things to be. This process works beautifully in organizations, and just as elegantly with people doing their own personal-growth work.

Cameron was tired of the pattern he had fallen into with all his personal relationships. He was in sales and wanted more success and less tension in dealing with people.

I gave him a large piece of paper, four feet by three feet. I had him draw a wall of equal-sized bricks.

"What is this?" he asked.

"It's your structure."

We had spent a lot of time exploring the beliefs and agreements that were holding him back. He told me that when he was a boy, his father would frequently come home intoxicated, hours after he was supposed to be home. His dad would miss dinners, school plays, and kids' baseball games. When he finally did come home, everyone was angry at him.

His dad took refuge in Cameron's room.

"You're my boy, aren't you?" he'd say and then fall asleep on Cameron's bed.

To keep the house from erupting into chaos, Cameron learned to play both sides: calm everyone down and convince his dad that he was his ally. This went on for years. Through that experience, Cameron developed an outlook of fear. He didn't feel safe in any kind of relationship. As he got older, Cameron developed many strategies, stories, and agreements to support his "not safe" point of view. Things like: *For me to feel okay, I need to make sure you are okay. For me to know you want to be with me, I need to say the right things and act the right way.*

Cameron thought a different outlook might work better and feel better. He decided his new belief would be: *I'm safe. I'm okay right now. I can just be me and I can trust me.*

Now he was ready for the next step.

"In the middle of every brick, write an agreement you want to make with yourself that supports your new belief," I said.

A few weeks later he came back with a list of agreements that he decided would support what he wanted to create and would be the guidelines for his actions and decisions.

"Here they are," he told me. "Let me read them to you.

"I used to filter everything through my old experiences. I know that many of my experiences have value, but just because something went wrong in a similar situation years ago doesn't always mean it will turn out the same today. So my first agreement is, I can focus my full attention on this moment and be open to whatever happens.

"My next agreement is, I'm not going to assume anything. Because I had this filter about what had happened before, I assumed a lot about what was going on, jumped to conclusions, and got worked up over nothing. It also kept me from being understood or understanding anyone else. Now I'm going to ask questions and not assume anything.

"Next, I have an old habit of saying yes when I really mean no. When I did that I got angry because I realized I had agreed to do something I didn't want to do. I'm not always aware of it, but sometimes I say yes so everyone will be happy. I guess I want to keep the peace . . . okay, and be liked, too. My new agreement is, no more toleration out of fear—saying yes when I mean no. If I'm going to do something, I'm going to do it because I have decided I want to, not because I'm afraid you won't accept me if I don't. Unless it's critical or an emergency, I know it's okay to say in a friendly way that I'd rather not.

"My next agreement is checking in to see how I feel. I forget to pay attention to what my gut is telling me. I'm going to remember to ask myself some important questions like: *What is going on with me? Does this feel good or is there something I'm not listening to?*

"And my last agreement is, I realize I have a *Cameron* story about everything and they have theirs. I bend reality in my own way and everyone is going to do the same thing, but in a different way. What they do or say is not necessarily about me. I don't have to take care of everybody so they are okay and I feel safe."

When Cameron finished I had a question.

"This is your framework of agreements for smoother relationships with other people—that was your assignment, right?"

"Yes."

"Will this work anywhere else in your life?"

He thought for a minute and then smiled. "It will work for everything."

People often come to me and want to talk about a specific problem they are having. They have a vague sense of being stuck and want a sounding board for some change they desire—in the work they do, in the way their relationships have always gone, in their financial situation, or where they are headed in the future. What is interesting is that they never find a solution looking at all the little details. There is a series of agreements about how things are that drives their choices. What's intriguing is how the structure of agreements supporting what they believe affects everything, not just what they came to talk about.

**The beliefs that hold up your framework
of agreements are threads that run through
your entire life, not just a part of it.**

And this is no different for an organization. When we are invited to work with a company, it's because of a disconnect between the mission of the company, its values (what its people would like to believe), and what is really happening day in and day out. Everyone is always focusing on a specific problem, but when we look at the real culture, what people say when they think they are free to talk, we typically find hidden limiting core agreements that affect everything.

Building a Framework of Agreements

Constructing a framework of agreements that supports what you want to achieve gives you a system to check in and weigh what you are about to do. The structure becomes a reliable filter for all your decisions. If you know what you want and what it is supposed to look like, then your framework should support that.

Besides defining the belief and the point of view you'd like to nurture, the most important part of developing a framework of agreements is knowing what outcome you'd like. An outcome can be your own reactions, the reactions of others, your attitude, how you feel, or a real event. Whatever outcome you get is feedback. If you like what you are getting, great! If you don't like what you are getting, then that is the truth, *but only in this moment.* No one is at fault, no one is to blame—the feedback says it all. Whatever you are doing isn't completely working, and whatever actions you are taking aren't giving you the results you want. So modify what isn't working and watch the feedback. If you need to, modify again, and again, and again. Do it until you get the results you are looking for.

One afternoon, I gave a talk in Southern California about designing a framework of agreements, and afterward a woman came up to me and asked, "Aren't these agreements just affirmations? I've tried affirmations and they never work."

Affirmations can be useful, but unless you address your underlying beliefs, they are a beggar's song—wishing, hoping, and praying. Designing a framework of agreements is not begging. Designing a framework of agreements to support a well-constructed belief is about authority and accountability. This is your creation. Deliberately assembling a matrix of agreements means you are constantly weighing what you are about to do against what you have decided you want.

In my own organization we have built a framework of agreements to help us make decisions about what to do. Again, this is no different from what has always gone on; there has always been some sort of network of agreements driving our actions. We have simply decided to notice this dynamic and use it to create the best life we can by consciously developing a group of agreements that supports our values. Holding our framework of agreements together is one covenant:

If any decision, action, or behavior cannot be accommodated into this framework, and does not conform to our stated values, we should seriously consider abandoning it.

To apply this covenant demands flexibility and common sense. For example, one of our values is that what we are involved in should feel good. To quote our framework of agreements: *The majority of the time the work should be uplifting, serve the community in a positive way, and promote personal growth and fulfillment.*

Now that's a tall order. Obviously, tedious work is sometimes required. If you love horses and riding horses gives you great joy, at the end of the ride you still have to brush down the horse, tend to the gear, put down food and water, and clean out the stall.

But from the perspective of our own internal agreement—*the majority of the time the work should be uplifting, serve the community in a positive way, and promote personal growth and fulfillment*—if what we have decided to do becomes chronically draining, creating constant drama and turmoil, we will seriously consider abandoning our approach, the not-doing of what we decided to do, and make a fundamental change.

When designing a new framework of agreements and trying it out, be patient. People often tell me that they have tried to map out what they'd like to achieve, designed a belief, and created agreements to support that belief, but the results were not what they expected.

After a little investigation I find that although they thought they were following a new pattern, they really weren't. Although they had an awareness of something they wanted to change, their actions were still supporting the old behavior.

I have lived in Colorado for more than 25 years. When I first arrived, a few friends took me skiing. They showed me some basic techniques and down the hill I went! I never took an actual lesson, and over the years I developed a lot of bad habits. So in the last few years I have been taking skiing lessons. Last year, one instructor pointed out a bad habit I have: holding my right hand behind me as I make a right turn. You are supposed keep your body facing downhill as you turn, with your arms bent at the elbow as if you are holding a tray, but my right hand was behind me throwing me off balance.

I practiced the new technique. The next time I met with the instructor she said, "Okay, let me see you ski." I skied in front of her very carefully, doing exactly what she had taught me to do the last time.

When we stopped she said, "You still have your right hand behind you."

I was surprised. I had been very careful not to do that.

"No, I don't," I said, flustered. "I was paying very close attention."

She stared at the ground and then slowly looked me in the eyes. "You can't see yourself but I can. You are still dragging that hand behind you."

She got a video camera and filmed me for the rest of the day. I was hyper-aware of what I was doing and sure I was getting it right. The next time we met for a lesson she showed me the film. What I thought I was doing was not what I was actually doing. I was still dragging my right hand behind me.

We are so close to our personal dream it's sometimes hard to step outside of it. Maybe we think we are aware of what we are doing but many times we are not, even if we are trying hard to change a pattern or a habit. So be patient! Ask other people to watch you and tell you what you are doing. Record conversations with people you find to be difficult. Mount a video camera in your office or in your kitchen. All that may sound a little weird, but it's an effective way to see if what you are doing is what you *think* you're doing. Carefully assemble a framework of agreements that supports what you want to believe, be honest and gentle with yourself, and practice, practice, practice. If you don't like the feedback you are getting, modify your approach and try again.

The Prime Directive
Is Not-Fear

ONE OF THE MOST POPULAR SCIENCE FICTION STORIES OF all time is *Star Trek*. The basic story idea is simple. In the far distant future, Earth has created a military and exploratory branch of the United Federation of Planets. Called Starfleet, it consists of spaceships that travel many times faster than the speed of light, explore unknown galaxies, and seek out life on new worlds. Each spaceship, called a starship, is a technological marvel with a large crew acting according to military protocol. Each member of the crew has a rank and clearly specified duties.

Many times these starships find themselves isolated and out of communication range with the highest authorities. Gene Roddenberry, the creator of *Star Trek*, had an intriguing idea. What if these space explorers encountered a situation that no one could anticipate? What if they found themselves in a totally unexpected predicament? Is there one all-purpose value, a foundation that can support all the rules and regulations aboard the ship, to guide them to the right decision no matter what they encounter?

The answer was found in the *Prime Directive*, a principle that all the rules and regulations of the ship could rest on. In an otherwise dark and confusing situation with no apparent solution, the prime directive was their guiding light.

The concept of a prime directive, not the actual order laid down in *Star Trek*, is what's interesting. The idea of a prime directive goes far beyond science fiction. Whether we notice it or not, every person, every organization, and every nation has one organizing principle that all their agreements, rules, and values rest on.

Every pact we make about who we are, what the world is, and what we can and cannot do—our personal framework of agreements—sits on a foundation composed of one principle, one belief that shows us the way us no matter what. This guiding principle can only serve one master.

**Your central and most core belief,
the one that supports all your other
agreements, serves either fear or love.**

Mary's husband left her for another woman. As a result of what happened, she has decided love hurts and will never fall in love again. She cooked for her husband, kept a nice house, mended his clothes, and cared for him when he was sick. In turn, she expected him to keep his end of the bargain and love her, but he did not—at least not forever. Now she can never forgive him and she has lots of stories to support her point of view—stories about what he did and didn't do, and how he's responsible for her problems. Her anger, however, doesn't serve the purpose she intended it for. It doesn't harm him or drive him to change; it's the way she abuses herself. She's made a series of decisions about what happened and over time adopted strategies to keep everyone at a safe distance. These are the agreements she's made with herself about what to do and what not to do. All her rules, stories, and agreements describe and defend the point of view of a belief she harbored long before she met him. Hidden far below the surface she had a secret fear and he resurrected it. Her deepest core belief, her prime directive, is clearly: *I'm not enough.* A belief that serves only one master. Fear.

If you consciously decide to construct a framework of agreements to support what you desire to achieve, make sure they reside on a firm foundation. Unreasonable fear, fear based on lies, or someone else's fear-filled opinions about who you are or what you should do is unstable and will crumble under pressure.

To have an unshakable foundation, build your framework of agreements on a foundation of love. Easy words to say, but not always easy to do.

What is real love, anyway? Is love the way you are supposed to treat your family, or the temporary madness that burns away after the lightness of falling in love fades? Beyond your closest personal relationships, how can you apply love to your work, the relationship you have with yourself, or the day-to-day events in an organization?

What we think is love is frequently not love at all. Often, what we consider love is actually fear. If you'll remember the story of the First Dream—our initial life-dream of how the world is tainted by the parasite of fear—love is a conditional agreement that says:

- *I will accept you if you do the right thing, say the right thing, and be the right thing.*
- *I'm responsible for your emotional well-being and, in turn, you are responsible for mine.*

So then, what is real love?

Real love is a force—the intent of Life—that is experienced, not manufactured, when you assemble your awareness at the point of no judgment.

We experience true love when we tune into its frequency by perceiving things with no judgments at all. The actual experience of love is sometimes difficult to explain in words, but easy to understand. Real love is simply *not-fear.*

We understand what fear is with much more clarity than we understand the true nature of love. Imagine for a moment that someone is rude to you. You struggle over how to handle the situation and come to me for counsel. I give you this advice: *Treat them with love.*

When this person is rude to you again, you remember my words but think, "How can I take his advice? The way she behaves hurts me. I want to get as far away from her as I can. I don't see how I can show affection or be friendly to someone who treats me this way."

Maybe the path to love (not-fear) is unclear and confusing in a situation like that but it's easy to notice the fear. Stripped of all the arguments about who is right and who is wrong, we know without thinking that this perspective is all about fear.

Emotional attachments like holding a grudge, feeling responsible for others' emotional well-being, being right, making assumptions, having big expectations, trying to control things, and the agreement—*I will accept you if you do the right thing, say the right thing, and be the right thing*—are all good examples of fear-filled behavior. This sort of fear is easy to recognize because of the emotions attached to it. Bottom line: it doesn't feel good.

Not-Fear

The opposite of baseless fear is not-fear. It's the *not-doing* of fear. Remember, not-doing is a decision you make to consider the opposite of what you have always been doing because that point of view may be worth exploring. Not-doing is about suspending judgment and stepping off the island of what you think you know to get a better view.

The not-doing of fear, when dealing with someone who is treating you badly, doesn't mean you approve of what they do, invite them to lunch, or go on vacation with them. It means you choose a personal posture and course of action that cherish and nourish your human being. You do it because the emotion feels good.

Not-fear might look like this:

Again, someone is rude to you and what she says doesn't feel good. Being offended doesn't feel good either. The emotion you feel moments before you launch into being offended is telling you the truth. The truth is: This is not-love. Her behavior comes from fear and that's useful information. The way she perceives you and acts toward you is fabricated in her own virtual reality. It's not personal.

Choosing not-fear is about being guided by the feelings that arise out of what you are about to do. No matter what you decide, give up being right because it manufactures emotional poison. You may be accurate (she is acting in a way that doesn't feel good to you), but judgment resulting from being offended, reacting, and igniting emotional turmoil is like eating garbage. It's emotional junk food that's not good for you. Choose a perspective that doesn't buy into the fear, take care of yourself, and do what serves your highest good.

You decide where to put the spotlight of your awareness, your attention. Wherever you put your attention establishes a discrete channel of communication and you *consume* whatever comes through the channel.

Aligning with not-fear and giving up the need to be right doesn't mean you forgo any action that is the obvious conclusion of being right. Acting from love doesn't mean becoming a doormat or letting yourself be abused. Do what you need to do; just move your attention away from any perspective that involves judgment and causes you pain.

Tess is a manager in a small marketing firm serving regional newspapers in rural Colorado. A graphic artist working for her had become a problem. He was late for work, argued with customers, and misread his assignments several times a week. Tess tried everything she could think of. She talked to him, sent him to a class to learn better tools for communication, explained the agreements he had to make to work there, and put him on probation. None of it seemed to work. She was enormously frustrated with his behavior and couldn't understand how anyone could be so blind, not seeing where this was leading and not doing something to stop it.

After several discussions with her boss about what to do next, Tess decided to fire him. But she couldn't stop thinking about it and was up all night, worrying. She called me, and after talking it through she realized why she was so emotionally drained. She was addicted to being right.

Tess was continually demanding that he *should* know what was going on and do something different, and she was offended that he didn't get it. That attitude was like having a little button on her desk marked "pain" and pushing it over and over and over again.

When she gave up her need to be right and approached the situation from a place of not-fear, she began to push the "pleasure" button. She felt at peace and secure in her decision. The action she needed to take was exactly the same as when she was right and feeling the pain of her judgments. He could not continue to work there because he couldn't keep the agreements he made when he took the job.

Another example of acting from the perspective of not-fear: Let's say you overreact to what someone says about you, and you have a big argument with them. Both of you are emotionally upset. After a few days of not sleeping well, you decide you were wrong and want to apologize. You don't like having someone mad at you, but you are worried about what to say.

What if they won't forgive me?

What if they don't like me anymore and it's my fault they're unhappy?

If you are responsible for someone else's emotional well-being, and believe the only way they will accept you is if you do the right thing, say the right thing, and be the right thing—that's a viewpoint ruled by fear.

The first step in choosing not-fear is to recognize how your actions leave you feeling. Perhaps your overreaction and the things you said have left you feeling uneasy and out of balance. But worrying whether they will ever forgive you doesn't feel good either! The act of not-fear is to treat yourself with love. Be impeccable with yourself. *Push the pleasure button!*

Clean up your mess. Go to them and apologize. Speak honestly about what you did and how you felt—never blaming them—and take complete responsibility for your actions. And one more thing: How they respond to your bad behavior, and your apology, is none of your business. They live in their own virtual world and will interpret and distort you in ways you will never completely comprehend. Whether they accept your apology or banish you forever has nothing to do with you. Clean up your mess and take action from the vantage point of not-fear. Treat yourself with love and push the pleasure button.

Just designing a new framework of agreements is not enough. They need to rest on a firm foundation; solid beliefs aligned with the intent of Life. Any set of agreements, any group of rules or values can be distorted to serve fear. The foundations of many of the world's religions rest on commandments that have been used for thousands of years to justify persecution and self-righteous violence, an injustice that goes on today, close to home and all around the world.

We are always looking for new solutions that will create a revolution in the way we live. Better, smarter, faster, and more efficient. But the real revolution will come when we routinely choose viewpoints that serve not-fear. That is what will change the world, our families, our relationships, and business in ways we can only begin to imagine.

**The prime directive of not-fear is a
lighthouse, a beacon in the fog that can
always guide you home. Use the prime
directive of not-fear to clarify and
cleanse every decision you make.**

Before you make any decision, speak, or take action,
remember the prime directive. Ask yourself this one simple yet powerful question: *Is this fear or is it not-fear?*

The Engine of Love

GARY ERIKSON IS THE CEO OF CLIF BAR, a company that makes energy bars, high-quality, healthy snacks favored by cyclists, hikers, and other athletes. In his book *Raising the Bar,* he writes about how he went from being broke and living in a rented garage with no bathroom or heat in Berkeley, California, to running a $120 million company in just 14 years.

A few years ago Clif Bar was riding a giant wave of success, but Gary was tired—stressed out from working too hard for too long. He decided to sell the company. His reasons had a lot to do with the engine of fear. He feared there wouldn't be enough money to keep on growing. He feared the company was becoming too big for his team to handle. He feared they wouldn't be able to compete with larger corporations, they would be crushed, and it could all be gone in an instant.

The day Gary went to sign the papers to sell the company, something came over him. His hands began to shake and he couldn't breathe.

Gary told everyone at the conference table he needed to

take a walk around the block. He hadn't been sleeping well for weeks and knew something inside him was trying to get out. He went outside and began to weep, and instantly he knew. He wasn't done with what he had started. He wanted to continue to build a business where people experienced work as a place to grow, express their passions, nurture innovation, and not just get a paycheck. And the product, besides being profitable, gave people a better life.

People thought Gary Erikson was crazy for not selling the company that day. He had given up an enormous pay-day for something intangible. As the president of a large, successful company, he did an extraordinary thing. He put reason, statistics, balance sheets, facts, and figures in their proper place and listened to his inner voice. He paid attention to the emotional messages he was getting, stayed balanced, and kept his creative life intact. He noticed that he was driven by fear, and refueled with what drove his passion and dedication in the first place. He replaced the engine of fear with an engine fueled by love.

Every action you take, large or small, mission-critical or merely routine, is a result of something that is driving you. What propels you forward is an engine injected with your ideas, experiences, expectations, opinions, beliefs, and personal agreements.

Fueling your engine with love simply means you choose compassion, discovery, and desire, counseled by the way you feel, as a way to embrace and welcome change.

Replacing the engine of fear with the engine of love is only possible if you agree that it's possible. When it comes to work, I talk to many people who tell me they have two lives. They have their personal life, passions, and spiritual predilection in a private world where they can be who they really are. And then there is work. At work you put on a thin mask, surrender to an unending and unsatisfying grind, put your head down, do what needs to be done, and don't bring your personal life into it.

Certainly there are many jobs that seem to demand this kind of two-separate-lives behavior. But these business cultures are communities created by agreement. If you encounter a profit-at-all-costs environment that runs on fear requiring you to abandon what feels right, and you agree to be there, then that is what you will get.

Some of the largest and oldest companies in the world were founded by people clearly driven by fear, ruthlessly abusing competitors and employees alike. But very quickly we forget. We worship roaring financial success, agree to buy their products, and in some cases even work for them. Everything we do is based on hundreds of agreements we make with ourselves. When we agree to business without consciousness, respect for the power of human assets, or social and environmental citizenship, and we assume the old way is the only way to make money, then that is what we will get.

The idea that we have two lives, a work life and a personal life that require two completely different sets of values, is nothing more than an agreement—an agreement steeped in fear that will never result in balance, growth of our spirits, or sustained well-being.

A Better Way to Make Decisions

One way to break the habit of accepting choices made by fear is to change the way you make decisions. What you agree to is what you decide. You make little decisions in every moment.

Sometimes we are faced with life-altering choices: what job to take; where to move; what school to choose; where to spend our money; whom to start a life with; when to start over. For some, big decisions are a struggle, littered with pro-and-con lists, restless nights, and endless worry. Fear is a parasite, remember?

When faced with a major decision, have you ever asked yourself: *What if I do the wrong thing? What if I make a* big *mistake?*

It's easy to see when the struggle is driven by fear.

Worry is a circular discussion in your mind. You go around and around looking over the same information, the same arguments. It's like being lost at night in an unfamiliar neighborhood circling in your car and only realizing you are lost after you pass the same house three times.

The circling process of decision-making is driven by the engine of fear—fear of not doing it right, fear of not doing what you are *supposed* to do, wanting to make everyone happy, or not wanting to be criticized. The engine-of-fear process of making decisions is all about avoiding pain. We think too much, go in circles, and if we feel uneasy about what we have decided to do, we may ignore our uneasiness or talk ourselves out of it.

There is a better way: Make decisions using an engine of love.

> **When you fuel your engine with love you recover your passion. That's because love is what excites you, makes you grow, delivers you into an expanding universe, and compels you. Love is what feels *right*.**

Before you make your next big decision, collect information and become informed. Then let your feelings guide you, and notice whether these feelings are emotions in the moment or emotions in memory. Remember, memories are often filled with lies about what is true right now. Use the technique: *Stop the World.* Put the question in your mind, let it go, and allow your dreaming mind to advise you.

Finally, love yourself without limits because whatever you decide, in that moment, you are doing the very best you can. You cannot possibly know exactly how things are going to turn out after every decision you make, so make your decision with the understanding that you will be okay with whatever happens. Let go of your attachment to an exact outcome. You grow and learn by each experience, so offer yourself unconditional acceptance for your decision.

Despite old habits, the engine of love compels us. Awareness of the benefits of changing fuels, from fear to not-fear, is occurring in some of the most unlikely places.

Growing tired of stories of companies obsessed with competition resulting in corporate corruption and collapse, consumers and investors alike are moving from being driven by price and profit to following their sense of purpose. Support is growing for organizations all over the world that aggressively pursue solutions that champion the human spirit. For example, a call is rising aimed at the producers of goods to reduce energy consumption, greenhouse gas emissions, air and water pollution, and waste from unnecessary packaging. Companies are made up of people, members of the community, and more and more are recognizing that in a global economy environmental problems and human problems are everyone's problem. The supply of products can only be sustained if the living Earth and its communities are revered and protected. Conscious companies that put these values into action are reaping rewards inside their organizations and at the cash register.

Architectural Energy Corporation in Boulder, Colorado, began 25 years ago with a single mission: to help the people who design, construct, and own buildings to use less energy and adopt more environmentally friendly practices. Their first customers were government research projects. The traditional building community considered their suggestions nothing more than an annoyance. Today, AEC has hundreds of projects all over the world and is growing at a staggering rate. The concepts of energy efficient design, aggressively using daylight to illuminate work spaces, creating healthy environments inside of buildings, and paying attention to pollution, recycling, and water use when constructing a building have become ideas that are catching fire.

CEO Michael Holtz: "Our business plan has always been T-I-G—*Trust in God*. We always felt good about what we were doing, and we attracted people who felt the same way. We were trailblazers, I guess. What was once thought of as a lofty idea, but not necessary, has now become an integral part of the decision-making process."

At hundreds of visionary companies like AEC, what was "the way we do business" is being transformed by carefully designed agreements with a new intent. This intent believes firmly that we have to consider people, the community, and the impact on the living Earth as an integral part of the decision-making process. That's fueling the engine with love.

**Fueling your engine with love means
making the perspective of not-fear an integral
part of every decision-making process.**

Individual spirituality, personal growth, and classic values are emerging as a new trend in the goods we buy, the way we use energy, our travel, and even in our justice system.

Justice in today's world is frequently about punishment: what crime was committed, who did it, what law was broken, and who will be punished for it. In our current model of justice, after an indictment, trial, and verdict, a court of law decides on the sentence—punishment as a penalty to even the score and scare the offender so they will think twice about ever committing a crime again. Being branded as a criminal means carrying a record that affects people for the rest of their lives. Our criminal justice system is supposed to be a deterrent, and yet there are more than 2 million people in prison in the United States alone, a number that is increasing each year. Our justice system, criminal and civil, is about winning and vindication, yet most of what the victim and the accused find in court is anguish, misery, and the reopening of old wounds. There is frequently no resolution in court, merely a judgment about who is right and who is wrong. Justice attempts to restore our happiness by hurting the person who wronged us, but the satisfaction doesn't last. This type of justice is all about fear. Its focus on vengeance is not all that different from some of the crimes themselves. Read any newspaper: The concepts of *justice* and *vengeance* are what spur the terrorists to terrorize.

A new model of justice is appearing in communities all over the world: *restorative justice,* restoring harmony to the community. In restorative justice, if the offender is willing to accept responsibility for their crime, a circle is assembled with the offender, the victim(s), members of the community, and a moderator. This model reflects ancient tribal methods of dealing with offenses to the tribe. Their idea was that when a crime is committed, harmony is disturbed, communication is broken, and the community is harmed. By letting offenders directly experience the effect of their behavior, and by allowing the victims to experience a declaration of responsibility by the offender, communication can be restored and repair of the harm can begin. Fixing the harm requires consequences the community will accept in order to move on. Sometimes the harm can't be completely repaired. If the crime involves a death, the harm to the victim is irreversible, but nonetheless, the process heals many wounds. Applied to the pettiest and most serious of crimes, when it works, restorative justice is a beautiful application of not-fear. When all the parties are in the circle, human to human, not blaming, shaming, vindictive, or demanding to be right, with a common goal of repairing the fabric of community, real magic can and does happen.

Because what you believe affects everything, without exception, you can apply the engine of love to any situation, any circumstance. And it changes everything.

One afternoon I was in a big city airport waiting for my connecting flight, and I went to get a hot cup of tea. I found a stand that sold coffee drinks and pastries, and waited in line for my turn. Behind the counter were three young Hispanic women making drinks, cutting cake, and taking money. They were working in a tight space and the line was long with weary travelers. What I noticed immediately captured my attention. The women behind the counter were smiling and singing. They moved in a continuous synchronized dance, like birds flying in a flock. They whirled around each other affectionately, efficiently taking care of customer after customer. I was so captivated by what I saw that after I got my drink I sat down at a table and watched them until it was time to catch my next flight. To be sure, their work was tedious and low-paying in hot cramped quarters, and yet they were laughing, joyful—even playful with each other and everyone who came up to the counter. I felt connected. It wasn't the kind of buying experience I have every day. It was an exquisite demonstration of taking action and meeting life, possessed not by the parasite of fear, but instead driven by an engine fueled with love.

The Myth of
Self-Improvement

POPULAR PSYCHOLOGY, YOU CAN DO IT! BOOKS, GLOSSY magazines all about Self, New Age mantras, along with an endless progression of television commercials, pound out the message, You can have it all! You can be happy, successful, attractive, and vibrant. You can have passion in your work, all the while tapping into an effortless, endless wellspring of energy. It sounds sooo good! Yet if you can't do it, after trying really hard, you may end up feeling like a self-help failure. All of this can leave you wondering, *What's wrong with me?*

Sometimes the quest for self-improvement, rather than making us feel better, leaves us feeling worse. At first exhilarating, as we continue to search for self-improvement, it can actually increase our stress and feed the belief we've been trying so desperately to get rid of. That awful belief, *I Can't.*

Part of the self-improvement mantra is manifestation. If I really, really believe it, if I sharpen my intent, I will manifest whatever I desire. And if I don't get what I want there *must* be something wrong with me.

When what you want doesn't appear in the way you expect, what gets sharpened is an old agreement:

Somehow I don't get it.

It will never happen.

I must be, in some way, defective.

Or perhaps you decide that all the "*You Can Do It!*" stuff out there is simply a quick way for some folks to make barrels full of money, and for most people it just doesn't work.

One woman wrote me, "I have such a strong positive belief about my success as a novelist that occasionally I wonder if I'm deluded. Meaning, the risk and reward of having gone through a lot of savings, *believing* it will come back in spades . . . spiritually and with real life security. I've worked so hard, and enjoyed it, but I need the rewards and recognition to prove to my family and friends that I wasn't crazy."

What struck me about her letter was the comment: *I have such a strong positive belief about my success . . . that occasionally I wonder if I'm deluded.*

I have talked to many people who have wholeheartedly adopted the idea of *I Can!*, gone way out on a limb—financially, physically, emotionally—and feel that if success doesn't come back to them in the way they expect it, they'll be very disappointed! At they same time they wonder: *Am I fooling myself?*

There is a hidden fear in this pattern, a monster of sorts hiding in the closet. What if it doesn't work out as expected?

If things don't work out as expected these people are often more than disappointed, they're devastated! Devastated because adopting the strategies found in personal growth manuals is a great strategy to avoid past pain.

Thinking that after all this time you have finally found something that will fix that real yet unnamed fear is intoxicating. Perhaps even a delusion because if you adopt the idea—*I Can!*—without ever changing the real beliefs you have about yourself, then the road to disappointment is well marked and heavily traveled.

If your pursuit of improvement rests on a bed of fear-based beliefs, it will only lead to more of the same. If the journey toward a higher level of functioning is driven by the engine of fear, then each turn in the road will be experienced through the same *less-than* outlook that initiated the trip.

Often the motive for self-improvement rests on one simple belief. A belief with agreements like:

I'm not okay as I am.

No one will accept me like this.

To be honest, I cannot accept myself like this either.

Buying into the myth of self-improvement is a protective story we tell ourselves that is a thin veneer easily torn by distress, disappointment, or perceived failure. The myth of self-improvement is self-rejection because its seed is the belief, *I'm not.*

I'm not is often the real belief driving us to change, a belief undeniably propelled by the engine of fear.

Everyone wants to be recognized for their achievements and acknowledged for the work they do, and hear that they are on the right track. We want to be nurtured, get compliments, and be treated with respect.

We want it, but we don't need it. When we need it, we act from desperation and become powerless hunting for the prize of acceptance and recognition. Any program of self-improvement that is infected with self-defeating beliefs, driven by an engine fueled with fear, is an all-out treasure hunt for the prize.

Instead of looking for the prize, be the prize. Loving yourself without judgment, without limits, is the gift you give yourself when you become the prize you have been seeking. Being the prize makes you compelling, draws more opportunity than you ever thought possible, and spawns beliefs that will take you exactly where you want to go.

The push to change is inevitable. We are alive and life is evolving and ever expanding. Life exists embracing the marriage of opposites, cleanly and without conflict.

Is it possible to rest in complete self-acceptance, totally comfortable with who you are, breathing out in total surrender to what is, and then with the next in-breath, be charged with the desire to create something different—an evolution of life?

Rather than toiling to improve what you believe is flawed, recognize and change the stories you tell about how you are not enough. You can't get any better than you are, you can't go to the store and buy what's missing, but you can always take a different action by believing something else about yourself. Something else that nourishes you and feels right. Self-love and dedication to the prime directive of not-fear are so much easier to adopt than being sharply focused on the often fruitless pursuit of self-improvement.

Instead of being obsessed with improvement, try cleaning up the stories you have about how you should be. Get rid of descriptions of better, worse, right, wrong. Use the integrity of your emotions to guide you into making decisions on how to proceed. Build a conscious framework of agreements that supports what you want to achieve. Let your engine for change be the engine of love, self-love, rejecting the lie that you are the special one who just can't do it, no matter how hard you try.

The ideas, practices, and advice found in personal growth writings are often wonderful and inspiring wisdom. Use them as a gift to yourself, not because you need to be fixed, but because you want to awaken and experience the pleasure of life in its fullest expression. Use them because you have decided you deserve only the best. Do it because it feels good!

Devour inspiring wisdom as an expression of the affirmation of Life that needs no improvement but is always changing, creating, and evolving, as it always has.

As it always will.

Life on Purpose

CAROLINE DOUGLAS IS A SCULPTOR FROM BOULDER, Colorado. One evening she volunteered to help decorate the high school gym for her daughter's graduation. She was taping decorations on the wall while another parent was hanging streamers from the rafters using a scissor-lift. Suddenly, the lift collapsed—hitting her in the face.

Caroline suffered a broken nose and sustained a severe head injury. The road to recovery was long and frustrating. As part of her healing process, she decided to rededicate herself to being a sculptor and take her art business to a new level. But she encountered many obstacles on the way.

"I can't seem to get noticed," she told me. "I want to be recognized for my work and I'm hitting a lot of resistance getting into the right galleries, bigger sculpture shows, or getting any attention from the art press."

I knew Caroline had a goal in mind, but I was curious about what hidden belief was driving her. As we talked about her desire to be recognized for the work she was doing, she began to discover what was driving her.

Every piece she made had to be perfect—it had to be good enough. She pored over magazines looking at others' work to get the right combination of texture and technique.

Worrying about being good enough wasn't limited to Caroline's artwork. It infected every part of her life. For one thing, she had gotten into the habit of taking care of everyone's needs but her own. Without question, she had the "disease to please."

"I think I do this so everyone will be happy and like me."

She paused and took a deep breath.

"Actually, I'm afraid they'll abandon me."

She got up and looked out the window.

"When I was a little girl I felt abandoned by my parents because they were too busy for me. Somehow, I abandoned me too. I didn't listen to my feelings and I didn't trust myself. I learned to be invisible. In the church I attended with my family it was considered selfish to have wants. I guess that's still with me because I feel a little ashamed searching for recognition with my art."

Caroline decided to start a different type of project. She didn't worry about the product and instead focused on the process. Nothing had to be perfect. She stopped looking outside for recognition and instead started looking inside.

For one entire year she made a piece of sculpture every day. Each day she asked: *Who am I today?*

She set the clock for 20 minutes and stopped sculpting when the alarm went off.

"I expressed what I felt that day, or dreamed the night before. I honored the movement of the year and the changes that occurred. I allowed extreme parts of myself to be seen.

"I had no goal like recognition or fixing myself. I allowed myself to be fascinated by the moment and forget the outcome. What I learned was amazing. I learned that by just showing up, doing the work, paying attention, and having the discipline to do it, I reaped benefits far beyond what I could ever imagine.

"I noticed a lot about myself. I wasn't sure I was good enough, I worried about what everyone thought, and I felt ashamed if I wasn't brilliant or original. I realized I had been trying to prove to myself I was good enough and I was manipulating a lot of things out of fear."

Seeing that gave her the power to choose something else: something else to believe.

"Wanting to further my career was a huge step in asking for what I wanted without apologizing. The art also became a healing tool, creating space for more self-love. It seemed the more I was able to express in my art, the more I was able to give myself permission to accept all the parts of me."

For Caroline, recognizing the agreements she had made with herself and about herself was a grand awakening.

"I no longer look outside to compare my art to another's or feel I need to apologize for my personal spiritual journey. The process showed me the power of discipline and that focusing my attention in a conscious way can have huge benefits. I know now that I have within me all I need. I'm okay, I can trust me and ask for what I want. I'm responsible for my dream and what that creates. And I see clearly now that self-love is the greatest gift of all."

Today, Caroline is setting up "The Wall" at her art shows—an exhibit showing the 365 pieces she created during that year. She's also teaching sculpture at a local university. Her work is getting attention and even creating controversy. The art press is beginning to notice and her sculptures are being shown in some of the West's finest galleries.

Caroline is consciously living life on purpose—with intent, passion, and a big *yes* propelled by an engine fueled with love.

"Everything is flowing. I can trust and not fret. Before I manipulated the outcome and felt stuck. Now I'm on fire! I feel like I'm just beginning. I have to say things are working a lot better. I have this feeling deep down inside that good things will happen . . . and you know what? *They do!*"

Through her journey Caroline rediscovered herself and her power. And perhaps she found something else a lot of us are looking for—true purpose.

What Is Your True Purpose?

Bubbling up through the desire to find personal happiness and success, as well as meaning and value in what you do, are a few intriguing questions:

Why am I here?
What's my purpose?
What is the right thing for me to do?
Do I have a destiny?

Everything you do is based on agreements you make. Remember, all of your actions and beliefs are choices. If you have agreements that are born out of fear, then the actions you take based on those agreements will be driven by the same fear.

Is your purpose to feel bad? No, of course not. If you touch a stove and burn yourself you will remember what happened and try not to do it again. If you attempt to hammer a nail, slip and hit your finger, and it hurts, you'll make a big effort never to do that again, either. It's common sense. But we don't seem to remember the pain caused by choosing emotional drama. We re-act, reviving the bitter taste of our favorite emotional flavor over and over again, as if our purpose in life were to suffer.

Perhaps our real purpose in life is not so much about what we do, but how we do it. What we do in every moment revolves around a bigger purpose. I think our true purpose is to act deliberately in not-fear, instructed by how it feels.

Our true purpose is to awaken and serve love.

Love is not-fear. Love is what excites you, makes you grow, delivers you into an expanding universe, and compels you. Love is what feels *right*. From that perspective you can choose hundreds, thousands, perhaps millions of paths to action—perfectly suited to the moment.

What is the right thing, the thing I am supposed to do—my life's purpose?

Do you have some grand purpose? Requiring the right purpose, the one correct path that you need to figure out, is a fear-driven idea. Instead of a purpose-driven life, how about a love-driven life?

To prosper you need a vehicle for your true purpose. Something to add value, apply your creative energy, and allow you to experience life. Things like the career you choose, having kids, traveling to see the world, creating a business, building something, service to the community, or getting an education. But that's not your real purpose, it's the expression of your purpose.

Choose what ignites your passion, turns you on, makes you laugh, inspires you, touches you deeply, tickles your curiosity, opens your heart, and propels you into new worlds. Life on purpose is simply taking all the elements of belief—intellect and awareness, intention and intent, emotion, and your ability to dream—and awakening to their immense power.

Seven Keys

What are the keys to unveiling your true wisdom? Are they things that are mysterious and beyond ordinary understanding? Can only a select few unlock the door that leads to the extraordinary power of belief?

That has never been my experience. My mentor, don Miguel, repeated one thing over and over. What he said was part serious, part joke, and part insult.

He'd say, "If I can do it, you can do it."

Then he'd pause, tilt his head, and with a devilish gleam in his eye he'd exclaim, "And if *you* can do it, *ANY-BODY* can do it!"

Don Miguel was a can-do mentor. Every time I saw him his message was the same. If I can do it, you can do it! Although he was a successful speaker and bestselling author, he disliked the label of guru. The message of the guru is: I can inspire you, but there is very little chance you will ever reach my level.

What is stopping you from taking charge of your BeliefWorks and living the life you dream of? Nothing! Over the years, however, I have noticed two simple things that keep people from completely changing any self-defeating belief that holds them back.

First, they can't quite let go of the belief. They concur with the concepts on how to do it, but their agreement to change is just a bargain. They insist they can give up the belief, but it has to be on their terms. They are aware of their old agreements and feel stuck in them but it's too risky to completely withdraw their full investment of faith.

Guess what? There is no bargaining! Until you give up your story about how it is and completely surrender your attachment to being right, you will never let go of the belief you're trying to change.

The second reason people can't change a limiting belief, despite all their hard work and good intentions, is that there is one more powerful agreement left to overcome. *They don't really believe they can do it.*

When we agree to that point of view—*I can't*—it hides all the secret keys from us. We wait for someone to rescue us but they never come. On a level far below what we are aware of we believe the guru story—*they can but I can't.* The real secrets of our astonishing natural abilities are forever concealed when, deep down, we don't believe we can do it. When we don't believe we can do it, it reveals we have agreed to one last lingering, devastating lie. *There is something wrong with me.*

The seven secret keys for unlocking the remarkable power of belief are not really secrets at all. They have not been deliberately hidden from knowledge, nor are they an unsolvable mystery. In fact, there is nothing contained in this book you didn't already know.

Many of the concepts contained in *BeliefWorks* were

revealed to my clients and me as we did the work. You could say they are my invention, but I see them as wisdom revealed, echoes of the One Mind that is in all of us, revelations that appear as insight when we show up in the present moment, open to the power of our true selves and our constant communion with Life.

Seven Keys for Unlocking the Power of Belief

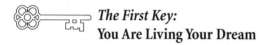

The First Key:
You Are Living Your Dream

Take full responsibility for your life-dream, and a world
of enormous possibility will open right before your eyes.

How can you discover the hidden beliefs that secretly impact your life?

Just look around you. You are the main character in your movie and many of the people you deal with on a daily basis are only minor characters reading from your script: a script with dialog and motivation supporting whatever you believe. To harness the force of belief requires awareness—awareness that you are living your dream and that whatever is consistently going on around you is not some odd coincidence or a run of bad luck.

What is keeping you from living your dream? Nothing!

It just isn't true that you are not living your dream. You are precisely living your dream. Seeing that without distortion opens a world of enormous possibility.

The Second Key:
Open the Gates of Lucid Living

> When you notice that everyday consciousness is
> awake-dreaming modified by the filter of all your
> agreements, the extraordinary magic of what
> you choose to believe will be fully revealed.

We create our personal dream of life using not only our language mind, but our dreaming mind as well. Past the words, our reason, and the things in life that are solid lies the unseen part of life that is fluid and mysterious. Unseating the ruler of the language mind and taking the steps to open true awareness—*perception without judgment*—throws open the gates of lucid living: being truly aware in your everyday waking life-dream. Lucid living cultivates clarity and engages the totality of all that we are: body, mind, and spirit.

The Third Key:
Balance the Four Elements of Belief

> The totality of who you are created the beliefs
> you are living, not just what you think is true.
> Balance those elements and the dream of your
> life will become your carefully crafted masterpiece.

The construction of belief is a holistic process, encompassing your whole human being. Belief is not just about what you think is true; it is a living dream with an emotional signature populated by agreements that define and defend its point of view. When you balance the Four Elements of Belief—Air: intellect and perception, Water: emotions in the moment and emotions in memory, Fire: intention and intent, and finally Earth: the dream and the dreamer—all the potential, all the possibility of belief is within reach.

The Fourth Key:
Design a New Framework of Agreements

Everything you do is based on all the agreements you have made with yourself. To support the beliefs you would like to have, design a new framework of agreements.

Rather than constructing a set of core values and never addressing the framework of agreements, personal or collective, that is operating powerfully and invisibly below the surface, take the time to discover what beliefs are running the show and design new agreements that support the outcome you want. Your structure should be a reliable filter for all your decisions. If you know what you want, then your framework of agreements should support that.

The Fifth Key:
Be the Prize

Instead of looking for the prize, be the prize. Being the prize makes you compelling, drawing tremendous opportunity, and spawns beliefs that will take you exactly where you want to go.

Everyone wants to be recognized for their achievements, acknowledged for the work they do, and hear that they are on the right track. We want to be nurtured, get compliments, and be treated with respect.

We want it, but we don't need it. When we need it, we

act from desperation; we become powerless hunting for the prize of acceptance and recognition. Any program of self-improvement that rests on a bed of self-defeating beliefs, driven by an engine fueled with fear, is an all-out treasure hunt for the prize.

Instead of looking for the prize, be the prize. Loving yourself without judgment, without limits, is the gift you give yourself when *you* become the prize you have been seeking.

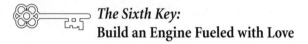

The Sixth Key:
Build an Engine Fueled with Love

Fueling your engine with love simply means you choose compassion, discovery, and desire, counseled by the way you feel, as a way to embrace and welcome change.

Every action you take, large or small, mission-critical or merely routine, is a result of something that is driving you. What propels you forward is an engine injected with your ideas, experiences, expectations, opinions, beliefs, and personal agreements.

Because what you believe affects everything without exception, you can apply the engine of love to any situation, any circumstance. By making this one agreement with yourself, you can change any event into an exquisite demonstration of taking action and meeting life, not possessed by the parasite of fear, but instead driven by an engine fueled with love.

The Seventh Key:
The Prime Directive Is Not-Fear

> The prime directive of not-fear is a lighthouse,
> a beacon in the fog that can always guide you
> home. Use the prime directive of not-fear to
> clarify and cleanse every action, every decision
> you make. Before you make any decision, speak,
> or take action, ask yourself this one simple yet
> powerful question: Is this fear or is it not-fear?

Whether we notice it or not, every person, every organization, and every nation have one organizing principle that all their other rules, agreements, and values rest on. Every pact we make about who we are, what the world is, and what we can and cannot do—our personal framework of agreements—sits on a foundation comprised of a single principle that shows us the way, no matter what.

Your central and most core belief, the one that supports all your other agreements, serves either fear or love.

If you decide to construct a framework of agreements consciously to support what you desire to achieve, make sure they reside on a firm foundation. Unreasonable fear, fear based on lies or someone else's fear-filled opinions about who you are or what you should do, is unstable and will crumble under pressure. To have an unshakable foundation, build your framework of agreements on a foundation of not-fear.

All the keys revealed here are simply an expression of the invisible intelligence that operates beneath the visible surface of life. An intelligence that is available to us when we let go of the pondering of our reason and avail ourselves of instant insight and intuition. An intelligence that is available to us when we embrace the ability of the mind to dream, in perfect balance with its extraordinary facility to reason with words.

Step off the island of what you think you know and many doors will open without a bit of struggle, revealing the extraordinary magic of what you choose to believe.

The Wizard of Kyushu Island

BELIEFWORKS EXAMINES, FROM MANY DIFFERENT ANGLES, the idea that what we believe deeply impacts our perception. But how do our thoughts and beliefs affect the physical world? Can belief affect matter itself?

It appears that our true power is the ability to affect what happens inside us rather than what happens outside us. We don't have ultimate control over physical reality or the people we encounter, but it is possible to deftly steer the hundreds of decisions and interpretations we make every single day.

In almost every case, the laws of the physical world dominate, no matter what we believe. My local newspaper, and probably yours too, occasionally runs a story about someone who is convinced he can fly, assisted by no more than an unwavering belief, and each time the force of gravity prevails.

And yet, there are numerous accounts of mind affecting matter, some thoroughly explained, some disputed, and some undeniably mysterious and, at first glance, unexplainable.

There is overwhelming evidence from scientists studying quantum physics that when experimenting with the
subatomic actions of earth's smallest particles, the
observer seems to affect the behavior of the experiment.
In tests using accepted scientific methods where the
results of carefully designed experiments are repeatable,
the power of thought and observation appears to cause
change to matter itself.

The mind-body connection in human beings is well
documented in both medicine and neuroscience. There
are thousands of examples about how thought and attitude invoke illness and can promote wellness. For example, numerous studies show that unexpressed outrage
results in an overabundance of stress-related hormones
depressing the immune system. Anger kept inside is
linked to migraine headaches, depression, insomnia,
back pain, heart disease, and ulcers.

False pregnancy (physiological changes that mimic an
actual pregnancy) and the phantom limb syndrome in
amputees (the perception of sensations in a missing arm
or leg) point directly to the incredible power of the mind
to impact the physical body.

The placebo effect is another excellent example.
When scientists give patients a dummy pill, saying that it
is the real drug to see how they fare, the patients frequently feel better. Doctors have long thought the effect
was purely psychological. Now, neuroscientists such as
Dr. Fabrizio Benedetti of Italy's University of Torino
medical school are finding direct evidence that the
placebo effect is physical.

Dr. Benedetti gave Parkinson's patients a placebo and
measured the electrical activity of individual nerve cells
in a movement-controlling part of the brain. Those neurons quieted down, a decrease in firing that reduced

patients' muscle rigidity and allowed them to move more easily. To further prove the power of belief, Dr. Benedetti hooked pain patients to a computerized morphine injection system. Sometimes the computer administered a dose without patients knowing it, and sometimes a nurse pretended to give it. Dr. Benedetti discovered that the morphine was up to 50 percent more effective when patients knew it was coming. Their brains immediately released more endorphins—chemicals that act as natural painkillers by blocking the transmission of pain signals between nerve cells—and they felt better.

Expecting a benefit can cause the same release of natural painkilling chemicals as the real drug. The placebo effect alters how the neurons in our brains fire, a measurable physical and psychological demonstration of the power of expectations.

Scientists are discovering that intelligence is located not only in the brain but in every cell of the body. The mind is non-localized. Our thoughts and beliefs not only have power over our bodies; they become our body. Thought and belief translate information into physical reality, between mind and matter, influencing both. These effects are so convincing that the National Institutes of Health, a renowned medical research center and agency of the Unites States Department of Health and Human Services, now houses the National Center for Alternative Medicine, a group studying the impacts on health of acupuncture, biofeedback, massage, meditation, visualization, and yoga.

Dr. Bruce Lipton is a former medical school professor, research scientist, and author of *The Biology of Belief*. As a college professor he taught what he had been taught, that your genes control all the biochemical events in your body and your DNA determines your health and behavior. The prevailing view when he was a graduate student was: Your fate is sealed, and you are at the mercy of your genes.

In a research experiment exploring the causes of the devastating disease muscular dystrophy, Dr. Lipton cloned human muscle cells and removed the nuclei from the cells with all the gene material. Without any genes to control the cell, it did the unexpected. *It acted like a normal cell.* It couldn't reproduce or repair itself, but it did function—without genes to instruct it on what to do.

What Dr. Lipton discovered is that cells are like computer chips: programmable biological matter. Our genes, our DNA are programs and our cells react not only from within but also from without. Cells respond to the environment they exist in. That environment not only consists of our fundamental biology but is also the expression of the way we live translated into biomatter. Our cells respond not only to biological programs but also to the program that runs our minds. That program is what we believe. Our perception of what is happening to us and around us influences the behavior of our cells. It's not always true that what is happening in our body is because we are victims of our genes. Sometimes we are the unwitting victims of what we believe.

What you believe dominates your attention, controls your behavior, and significantly impacts your biology.

Beyond what science has documented about how thought and emotion cross the physical world, millions of people have reported mystical phenomena that defy rational explanation—miracles of prayer, healing, and grace, eyewitness accounts of mystics in India performing astounding feats of mind over matter, and shamans in the jungles along the Amazon River summoning the weather. I myself have witnessed continuous synchronicity, miracles, and what can only be described as magic for which I have no reasonable description. I have also experienced darkness, pain, and unfortunate events that were, on closer examination, the unmistakable manifestation of where I had invested my own power of belief, my faith. For me, all of this poses one simple and yet enormously important question:

If you can affect your perception, your biology, and even matter by what you believe, what is possible beyond what you think is possible?

In Fukuoka, a Japanese city six hours southwest of Tokyo on Kyushu Island, there is a small restaurant called The Magic Parlor.

The owner of The Magic Parlor is called Hesamura. He is known as the Wizard of Kyushu Island because, as legend has it, he performs real magic.

Part entertainer, part psychic, Hesamura combines what appear to be normal magic tricks with feats of psychokinesis (the ability to affect physical reality with the power of thoughts). Hesamura doesn't charge for his show but insists you buy something to eat.

During his show, Hesamura bends objects like spoons, bottles, and coins right in front of the customers' eyes. He stretches bottles, which become a few inches longer. The elongated bottles then become part of the restaurant's display of Hesamura's magic feats.

In his performance he claims to mentally imprint pictures on Polaroid film. By one eyewitness account, he asked two men in the audience to pick cards from a deck, so only they could see the faces of the cards. He then instructed them to put the cards back into the deck. Next, Hesamura took one Polaroid photo of each of the men. When the photos were developed, the card they had each picked was superimposed on their faces. Also, there was an image of a dog next to the head of one of the men, and a little girl near the head of the other. These images turned out to be a former pet of the first man, and the daughter of the other.

Customers have witnessed Hesamura bending coins and making them go through yen notes. He also makes yen notes balance at the end of his finger, and then they suddenly float through the air and fly around his body. One evening he set clocks to a certain time, put the clocks in a bag on the counter, and then asked a woman in the audience to tell everyone the time she was born. When he took the clocks out of the bag in front of everyone, the time on every clock matched her birth-time exactly.

Hesamura also has a trick where he makes the hands of a wristwatch spin around. Simply by cupping a customer's watch in his hands, he makes it move forward precisely one minute. Then he cups it in his hands again and it moves forward exactly one hour.

Hesamura has been filmed by Sony Corporation's Extra Sensory Perception and Excitation Research Laboratory (ESPER) and by other paranormal researchers. To this day, no one has found a rational explanation for every trick he performs.

Hesamura claims he started as a boy trying to move insects with his mind. He practiced every day and after a few years he began to see real results. "Anyone can do this with practice," he says.

At the end of each show Hesamura gives a short lecture about how our thoughts affect reality. He admonishes the dinner crowd, "Pay attention to your thoughts!"

When asked how he can do what he does, Hesamura simply replies, "Because I believe I can."

So, How Is Your Dream?

THE LAST TIME I WENT TO VISIT DON MIGUEL, he was sitting on a big red couch, relaxing, upstairs, at his teaching center in California.

He had a life-threatening heart attack in the spring several years ago and so he takes it easy these days. Rather than getting up to greet me, he smiled with a bright gleam in his eye and extended his arms outward, inviting me to come and sit with him. I did so and he gave me a warm and wonderful embrace. We smiled at each other, taking in the moment, and then he asked me, "So, how is your dream?"

I stammered something silly as a reply, but the question stayed with me long after the visit was over.

So, how is your dream?

It wasn't the standard greeting most of us recite when we see a friend. He didn't say, *How are you? What's going on? How is the family? . . .* or anything like that. He asked me one very simple yet intriguing question . . . *so, how is your dream?*

What he asked in those five simple words was what he tried to teach me in all the years I spent with him.

You are completely accountable for the virtual reality that lives in your head. You have power beyond what you know. Everything you do is based on a framework of agreements that you assembled. You are living your dream. You are an artist of Life, and your actions, reactions, and the fabric of what you have agreed to believe are the culmination of your art up to this very moment. Your masterwork. You are, whether you are aware of it or not, the sole operator of your BeliefWorks.

And so, how is it going?

How is your dream?

The biggest adventure you can ever take is to live the life of your dreams.

—*Oprah Winfrey*

Stop the World

Each day rushes on with more to do than there is time to do it. A perpetual merry-go-round that never stops so you can get off. What would happen if you were to suddenly stop the world—even for just a few moments? Better yet, what would happen if you stopped your interpretation of everything, allowing yourself to observe your personal universe without its habitual lens of belief? What you might see is a new world of possibility without the story; your story of how things are.

To stop the world is to practice awareness and, for just a moment, surrender the description of everything you see that keeps your attention occupied.

Sit someplace quietly where there isn't anyone around to disturb you; somewhere you feel safe. Take off your shoes. Sit up straight. Don't cross your legs. Rest your hands on your thighs. Get comfortable and then make an important agreement with yourself: *I won't move.* When you shift your body, you give away your will.

Your inner dialog has your attention much of the time and so when you sit down to be still, there will be a war for your attention. Your mind will suggest that you fidget, scratch, or get up and write a note about something you might forget. To strengthen your will, don't move at all.

Just breathe. Slowly. Follow your breath with your attention. Breathe in through your nose slowly, imagining you are pulling air in from all over your body. Breathe out through your mouth, making the sound of the ocean or the wind. The in-breath is the will deliberately directing your attention as choice. The out-breath is letting go, releasing everything.

As you breathe in, let your body expand. As you breathe out, let your awareness expand. Notice how you feel, in your emotions and in your body. Resist the temptation to describe this to yourself in words. Just be aware with no attempt to define it or explain it.

Start by practicing 15 minutes each day, several times a week. Exercise this new habit. If you lose your attention to the chatter in your mind, don't make yourself wrong. Just refocus. Find the space between the thoughts. Be kind to yourself. There is no such thing as doing it right.

Glossary of Terms

Agreement: A bargain, a deal; a pact you make with yourself. Also, a contract that defines and defends the point of view of a belief.

Alchemy: The quest to transform lead into gold using the Philosopher's Stone. However, transforming lead into gold to obtain riches was a ruse used to protect its true powers. The Philosopher's Stone was actually a magical substance thought to cure illness, prolong life, bring about personal growth, and—at the height of its powers—lead to spiritual enlightenment.

Attention: The focus of your awareness, a searchlight scanning what is before you. Attention opens your perception to what is going on all around you and inside you. Where you place your attention opens a channel of communication with what is going on outside you as well as inside you. You learn and gather knowledge only by focusing your attention.

Awareness: Perception without judgment.

Belief: A living dream with an emotional signature populated by specific agreements that define and defend its point of view.

BeliefWorks: The human belief factory, fashioning a personal dream of life that touches every word we say, every thought we think, and every move we make. Our private BeliefWorks manufactures the prism through which we see life and magically transforms "what is" into what we *believe* it is.

Dreaming Mind: The part of our mind that perceives without words and records an impression of the inexpressible essence of the moment.

Emotion in Memory: The emotional point of view of a past pivotal experience. When the event happened, the emotion associated with your experience was telling you the truth. If that memory is triggered by something in this moment, the emotion that arises is often full of lies.

Emotion in the Moment: The intelligent response from our membrane of feeling, full of key information, that is always telling us the truth.

The Engine of Fear/The Engine of Love: Every action you take, large or small, mission-critical or merely routine, is because something is driving you. What propels you forward is an engine injected with your ideas, experiences, expectations, opinions, beliefs, and personal agreements. The fuel for that engine is either love or fear.

The First Dream: In order to pass information on to us when we were children, the adults needed to capture our attention. For this purpose they taught us language. Once we understood the code, they could tell us about everything they knew. This process of capturing our attention for the first time creates, by agreement, our initial life-dream of how the world is.

Framework of Agreements: Every action we take is filtered through a matrix of past personal agreements. Our reactions, and the decisions we make, are deeply impacted by the agreements we have made with ourselves that define and defend what we truly believe.

Intent: Intent is *what you mean to do*. Intent is a moving force always preceding someone or something in action. Intent is not a mental decision, yet it is initiated by a mental decision—your intention. Life uses the force of intent to manifest itself. You use the force of intent to manifest your own life, which includes assembling all of your beliefs. Every act of creation is intent followed by action.

Intention: Intention is the intellectual portion of action. What you intend to do is what you have "in mind." Intention is your mental agreement about how to proceed, a determination propelling you toward some action, some purpose in the moment.

The Island of the Known: Your own personal island of safety constructed of your beliefs, other people's opinions, all your knowledge, concepts, and experiences. It is the result of what you have agreed to and invested your faith in. It is the container of "me" bounded by what you believe.

Language Mind: The language mind is your reason, the ability to use words to analyze, assess, and judge what your tools of perception notice.

Love: Real love is a force—the intent of Life that is experienced, not manufactured, when you assemble your awareness at the point of no judgment. Real love is simply *not-fear*.

Lucid Dreaming: Lucid dreaming occurs the instant you recognize, while asleep, that you are dreaming. In the moment you realize you are dreaming, you become lucid and clear about what is happening. Lucid dreamers, unlike normal dreamers, can make choices in the dream.

Lucid Living: The practice of becoming aware, while you are awake, that you are dreaming all the time, modifying what you perceive through the lens of your beliefs.

Mitote (pronounced mih-TOE-tay): A voice of knowledge filled with judgments that has our attention most of the time. A never-ending clatter drowning out the essence of the moment.

Nagual (pronounced nah-WAHL): From *Nahuatl*, a language spoken by the people of Teotihuacán in Central Mexico: Nagual is the spirit that dreams, inhabiting the rocks, the plants, the creatures, and the humans. Everything that has a form emerged from a place of potential without form, nagual. Nagual is one-half of the reality we live in, half of our own nature. Also means teacher of Toltec Wisdom.

Not-Doing: Not-doing is a decision you make to consider the opposite of what you have always been doing because that point of view may be worth exploring. Not-doing is about suspending judgment and stepping off the island of what you know to get a better view.

Not-Fear: The opposite of baseless fear is not-fear. It's the *not-doing* of fear. Not-fear is real love.

The Parasite of Fear: If any part of our system of beliefs is infected with limiting fears about life, then those beliefs become a parasite depleting and draining us. If our awareness is overwhelmed by beliefs born of unfounded fears, we create a separate virtual reality that becomes a destructive force keeping us trapped, robbing us of our energy, and blinding us from truth.

Prime Directive of Not-Fear: Every pact we make about who we are, what the world is, and what we can and cannot do—our personal framework of agreements—sits on a foundation comprised of one principal, one belief, that shows us the way no matter what. The prime directive of not-fear is a lighthouse, a beacon in the fog that can always guide you home. Using the prime directive of not-fear will clarify and cleanse every action, every decision you make.

The Prize: Getting what you think you deserve: attention, acceptance, recognition, and the biggest prize of all—love.

Quetzalcoatl (pronounced ketz-ah-KWAH-tall): *The feathered serpent.* The would-be king of the Toltecs. A shining spiritual leader, god of intelligence descended from the Sun, and Christlike figure to the ancient Meso-American world.

Tenochtitlán (pronounced tea-nooch-teet-LAHN): The fabled capital city of the Aztec (now Mexico City).

Teotihuacán (pronounced tay-oh-tea-wah-KAHN): A pyramid city built by the Toltec approximately 2,000 years ago in the high midlands of central Mexico. The Toltec constructed the citadel of Teotihuacán, *The Place Where Humans Become as God,* as a place for community, a ceremonial seat of power, and a school for bringing selected groups of apprentices to personal freedom.

Tezcatlipoca (pronounced tess-SCOTT-lee-poh-cah): *The Smokey Mirror.* A mysterious god of the ancient Meso-American world originating from the night sky. A wizard appearing frequently as a shape-shifter, trickster, or magician.

Three Masteries: Three layers of understanding taught by the teachers of Toltec wisdom—the naguals—on the path to personal freedom. The Mastery of Awareness, The Mastery of Transformation, and The Mastery of Intent.

Toltec: An ancient culture that thrived in what is now the pyramid ruins of Teotihuacán in the high midlands of

Mexico. Not specifically a race or a religion, they practiced a unique way of life and were considered by the
farmers and artisans of the area to be men and
women of knowledge. They taught that there's no way
for us to change unless we have an awareness of how
we create our unique perception of the world. The
Toltec description of the human being is that the
mind is alive, and one of its main purposes is to
dream. They concluded we are dreaming 24 hours a
day and that we dream through the filter of our
beliefs about everything.

Tonal (pronounced toe-NAHL): From *Nahuatl*, a language spoken by the people of Teotihuacán in
Central Mexico. Tonal is all the things that make up
the solid, everyday world; things that can be named,
everything that has a form.

Tools of Perception: All the natural elements of human
perception: emotion; the physical senses of sight,
taste, touch, hearing, and smell; and the focus of our
awareness, our attention. It is through the Tools of
Perception that we perceive the world and construct
our filter of belief.

Totality of the Human Being: We are so much more than
just our bodies and our minds. In the cosmology of
the Toltec we are *tonal*—a form in the solid, everyday
world. We are *nagual*, the spirit that dreams, awareness inhabiting a human body. We are both the dream
and the dreamer. We are a marriage, a blending of
opposites.

About the Author

In 1996, after a chance meeting at the pyramid ruins in Teotihuacán, Mexico, Ray embarked on a six-year apprenticeship with don Miguel Ruiz, M.D., author of the international best-seller *The Four Agreements.*

Now CEO of EverydayWisdom.us and BeliefWorks.net, Ray has helped hundreds of individuals and businesses forge new beliefs and agreements to effect lasting and positive change. Before becoming an author, Ray was a professional musician, engineer, and a corporate executive for a nationwide facilities company with more than one billion dollars in annual sales.

In addition to his mentoring practice, he teaches seminars about BeliefWorks, and applying the age-less wisdom of the Toltec to life and business, throughout the United States and abroad.

If you would like Ray Dodd to speak at your next public event, association conference, or meeting, please contact us at: info@everydaywisdom.us.

EverydayWisdom
and BeliefWorks

Real Change—One Belief at a Time.

EverydayWisdom.us and **BeliefWorks.net** are organizations dedicated to assisting individuals and businesses in identifying the beliefs and agreements that present obstacles to getting the results they want. Once any self-limiting beliefs are identified, we facilitate the creation and integration of a new framework of empowering agreements, unleashing the potential for profound personal and workplace transformation.

For more information about one-to-one mentoring, seminars, classes, journeys, products, and programs, please visit our websites: www.everydaywisdom.us and www.beliefworks.net, or contact us at: info@everydaywisdom.us.

BELIEFWORKS™ is a registered trademark of EverydayWisdom.us Inc.

Acknowledgments

My sincerest appreciation to the BeliefWorks mentors who use these ideas to guide themselves and others to personal freedom: Thomas Gruner, Michelle Laub, Susan Marshall, Crystena Mikles-Gilliland, Massimo Perucchini, and Joe Scott.

To my advance readers whose time and feedback are greatly appreciated: Fred Dearborn, Carolyn Kesteuson, Susan Marshall, Professor Alan Nordstrom, Michael Racosky, Susyn Reeve, Beverly Title, and Marti Woodward.

My heartfelt gratitude as always to don Miguel Ruiz.

A special thanks to Bill and Ming at Waterside for their guidance, and to Bob Friedman and all the wonderful folks at Hampton Roads Publishing for their hard work in bringing this together.

Finally, my love and gratitude to all those who have supported this work and who were each, in some way, instrumental in developing the ideas found in this book. A partial list includes: Patricia Aburdene, Eileen Alm, Tim Bagot, Brian Bensen, Terry Black, Will Bledsoe, Ted Brassfield, Jyoti Caroline, Keith Carter, Evan Cummings, Caroline Douglas, Mitchell Dozor, Samie Dozor, Barbara Emrys, Shari Errickson, Elena Fong, Donne Fregeau, Joe

Gaffney-Brown, Rebecca Gaffney-Brown, Sam Garcia, Simeon Hein, M. M. Horton, Lydia Jandreau, Karen Keiger, Donna Krebs, Kit Kyle, Bren Lane, Dawn Link, Bruce Lipton, Joshua Martin, Neil McLane, Janet Mills, David Mitchell, Luis Molinar, Brandt Morgan, Darryl Morgan, Jill Musser, Bradley Myers, Dr. Gene Nathan, Steve and Heather Negler, Wendy Newman, Jeff Offsanko, Emily Palko, Dawn Pare, Larry Ransom, Dr. Tom Roberts, Nancy Ropel, Sheri Rosenthal, April Rothleutner, Phillip Rowland, Stewart Sallo, Eric Sanderson, Raka Satori, Simone Shipp, Barbara Simon, Grethe Skjolde, Marion Smith, and Chris Stambouli.

HAMPTON ROADS
PUBLISHING COMPANY, INC.

Thank you for reading *BeliefWorks*. Hampton Roads is proud to publish an extensive array of books on the topics discussed in this book—topics such as self-help, personal transformation, motivation, and more. Please take a look at the following selection or visit us anytime on the web: www.hrpub.com.

The Power of Belief
Essential Tools for an Extraordinary Life
Ray Dodd

Continuing in the tradition of the best-selling *The Four Agreements,* Dodd's first book reveals how our hidden beliefs create barriers to success and true happiness. An inspiring guide based on everyday wisdom, personal life coach Ray Dodd outlines four simple steps you can take to recreate any belief that stands in your way.

Trade paper • 152 pages • ISBN 1-57174-404-5 • $14.95

Excuse Me, Your Life Is Waiting
The Astonishing Power of Feelings
Lynn Grabhorn

Ready to get what you want? Get this—hard work and positive thinking can't do it alone. Lynn Grabhorn introduces you to "The Law of Attraction" and uncovers the hidden power of positive feeling. Now in paperback, this upbeat yet down-to-earth book reveals how our true feelings work to "magnetize" and create the reality we experience.

Discover the secrets that have made *Excuse Me* a **New York Times** bestseller!

Paperback • 320 pages • ISBN 1-57174-381-2 • $16.95

Mr. Everit's Secret
What I Learned from the World's Richest Man
Alan H. Cohen, author of *The Dragon Doesn't Live Here Anymore*

Mr. Everit's Secret is a modern-day parable examining our preconceived notions about happiness. When the story's narrator is hired to manage Mr. Everit's factory, he soon finds he's taken on not only a new job, but also a boss who seems bent on rearranging his entire belief structure. Mr. Everit imparts important lessons about overcoming fear and self-defeating modes of thinking, and taking care of people while letting life take care of you.

Hardcover • 120 pages • ISBN 1-57174-416-9 • $16.95

Before You Think Another Thought

An Illustrated Guide to Understanding How Your Thoughts and Beliefs Create Your Life

Bruce I. Doyle, III

Doyle's down-to-earth wisdom illuminates a way to change your life. By understanding how thoughts and beliefs affect your experiences, you'll have the key to designing a richer, more fulfilling life without limits.

Paperback • 128 pages • ISBN 1-57174-076-7 • $11.95

The Invisible Path to Success

Seven Steps to Understanding and Managing the Unseen Forces Shaping Your Life

Robert Scheinfeld

A noted motivational speaker lays out the seven key steps to identifying and working with your inner wisdom and passion to help create the life you want and need.

Paperback • 160 pages • ISBN 1-57174-358-8 • $14.95

Igniting the Soul at Work
A Mandate for Mystics
Robert Rabbin

A business consultant with spiritual roots shows you how to look beyond the drone of daily work life to find your own true inner vision and bring it to the workplace to transform your life and those around you.

Paperback • 160 pages • ISBN 1-57174-271-9 • $15.95

The Cosmic Ordering Service
A Guide to Realizing Your Dreams
Barbel Mohr

Best-selling German author Mohr teaches you how to fulfill all your wishes—just by placing an order with the universe. Learn how she used the Cosmic Ordering Service to gain her dream job, ideal mate, money, and even a castle to live in. Once you start using the Cosmic Ordering Service, the hardest part will be deciding what to ask for next!

Paperback • 112 pages • ISBN 1-57174-272-7 • $13.95

Smile for No Good Reason

Lee L. Jampolsky, Ph.D.

Recapture the joy of living! *Smile for No Good Reason* shares the twelve principles of Attitudinal Healing, a movement designed to show us how to achieve lasting happiness without having to change our social status, religion, or income bracket. Dr. Jampolsky shares powerful, heartfelt stories that show how to exchange fear for love, selfishness for service, and anger for clarity.

Paperback • 256 pages • ISBN 1-57174-415-0 • $14.00

www.hrpub.com · 1-800-766-8009

Hampton Roads Publishing Company

. . . for the evolving human spirit

HAMPTON ROADS PUBLISHING COMPANY publishes books on a variety of subjects, including metaphysics, spirituality, health, visionary fiction, and other related topics.

For a copy of our latest trade catalog, call toll-free, 800-766-8009, or send your name and address to:

HAMPTON ROADS PUBLISHING COMPANY, INC.
1125 STONEY RIDGE ROAD • CHARLOTTESVILLE, VA 22902
e-mail: hrpc@hrpub.com • www.hrpub.com